Early Christian Worship

Early Christian Worship

A basic introduction to ideas and practice

Paul Bradshaw

First published in Great Britain 1996
Society for Promoting Christian Knowledge
Holy Trinity Church
Marylebone Road
London NW1 4DU

Second impression 2000

This book was first published as
What Do You Mean By This Service?
by The Department of Church History at the
University of South Africa in 1995.

Extracts from R. C. D. Jasper and G. J. Cuming (eds)
Prayers of the Eucharist: Early and Reformed
(3rd edition 1987) are reproduced by permission of
Pueblo Publishing Company, New York.

British Library Cataloguing-in-Publication Data
A catalogue record for this book is available from
the British Library

ISBN 0–281–04930–0

Printed in Great Britain by
Biddles Ltd, *www.biddles.co.uk*

Subsequent digital printing in Great Britain by Cambridge University Press

Contents

Abbreviations

AIR   Edward Yarnold, *The Awe-Inspiring Rites of Initiation* (St Paul Publications, Slough, England 1971).

AT   *Apostolic Tradition* attributed to Hippolytus; page nos. are to the English translation by G. J. Cuming, *Hippolytus: A Text for Students* (Grove Books, Nottingham 1976).

DBL   E. C. Whitaker, *Documents of the Baptismal Liturgy*, 2nd edn (SPCK, London 1970).

PEER   R. C. D. Jasper & G. J. Cuming (eds.), *Prayers of the Eucharist: Early and Reformed*, 3rd edn (Pueblo Publishing Company, New York 1987).

Introduction

This book was originally commissioned as an undergraduate textbook for the University of South Africa and is now offered to a wider audience. It aims not merely to describe *what* rites Christians performed during the first few centuries of the Church's existence but also to explain *why* they did them: What caused them to choose those particular liturgical forms instead of others? What did they understand themselves to be doing in their worship? What effect did that have on the development of Christian doctrine? And how did new doctrinal formulations in turn affect the character of the rites? If readers keep these questions in mind as they go through each chapter, they should have little difficulty in finding the answers in the text.

In such a small volume it has not been possible to deal with the subject in great detail. Nevertheless, even though it has been necessary to tell the story in simple terms, the account has tried to remain faithful to the most recent historical scholarship, and nearly all the chapters conclude with some suggestions for further reading. More extensive background to the sources and methods used in the study of early Christian liturgy can also be found in my book, *The Search for the Origins of Christian Worship* (SPCK, London & Oxford University Press, New York 1992).

Paul Bradshaw

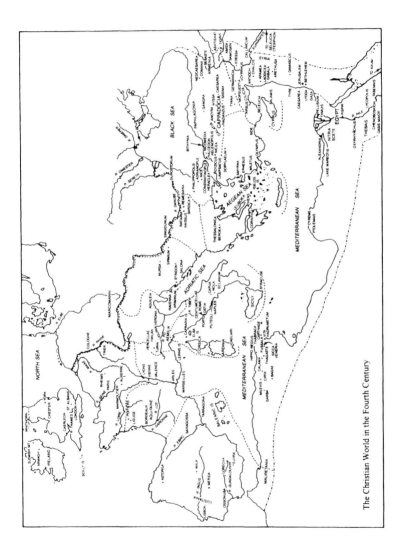

The Christian World in the Fourth Century

CHRISTIAN INITIATION

In this section, we shall first examine the roots of Christian baptismal thought and practice in New Testament times, and then see how different elements of this were picked up and developed in various early Christian traditions, concentrating principally on the contrasts between Syria and North Africa, before going on to look at the movement towards a more common baptismal theology and liturgy in the fourth century. We shall end our survey by considering the effects that the later spread of infant baptism had on both the practice and understanding of Christian initiation.

1. Beginnings

Jesus apparently did not leave his followers with a fixed set of doctrines but rather with an experience that changed their lives, which they then tried to articulate in their own ways. As a result, what we find in the New Testament is not one standard theology of baptism or a systematized explanation of what it means to become a Christian, but a variety of ways of speaking about that experience, quite different images and metaphors being employed by different writers in their attempts to communicate it to others.

Antecedents

The New Testament implies that the custom of baptizing those who were converted to the Christian faith was derived from John the Baptist (see, for example, Matt. 3.1–12), but the source of his own practice is uncertain. Some scholars have argued that it was based on the ablutions of the Jewish Essene community at Qumran, but these were repeated washings related to the need for constant ritual purity and do not seem to have included an initiatory baptism. Others have suggested that John was influenced by the practice of baptizing new converts to Judaism, but there is some doubt whether this was being done in his time or whether it was only adopted at a later date. A third possibility is that it arose out of the Israelite traditions of ritual purification (see, for example, Lev. 15.5–13) and/or of prophetic symbolism, which had spoken of God's people being cleansed with pure water in preparation for the advent of the messianic age (see, for example, Ezek. 36.2–8).

Whether the Christian adoption of baptism began with Jesus himself or only in the Church after his resurrection cannot easily be resolved. All three synoptic gospels record Jesus' own baptism by John but say nothing of him baptizing his followers. The Gospel of John, on the other hand, does not mention Jesus being baptized but does speak of him baptizing others (John 3.22, 26; 4.1; but cf. 4.2). Matt. 28.19–20 contains a command to baptize all nations, but there are difficulties in accepting this as an authentic saying of the risen Lord.

Baptismal practice

Whatever its origins, however, it appears that at least in certain Christian communities from early times it became the custom to initiate new converts into the Church through a process which included baptism in water. Unfortunately, the New Testament offers very few clues as to the manner in which the baptisms might have been carried out. The preference for the use of 'living' (i.e., naturally flowing) water that is found in some later sources (see also John 7.38) suggests that they may at first have usually been performed in a river or pool, where possible, rather than in a domestic bath-house. The image of baptism as participation in the death and resurrection of Christ used by Paul (see Rom. 6.3ff.) seems naturally to imply that candidates would have been totally submerged in the water, but such a practice would certainly not have been easily possible in domestic baths, and the custom found later in some places of candidates standing in a shallow font and having water poured all over them may also have existed in the earliest times. Both methods involved total immersion in water—it was only the way of achieving it that differed.

What else besides the actual immersion might have been involved is not made explicit in the New Testament. We would expect there to have been a preliminary period of instruction in the faith, at least in the case of Gentile candidates who lacked the religious background possessed by Jewish converts, but this need not have been the extensive formal catechumenate (from the Greek word *catechumen*, 'learner') found in later centuries. Several New Testament passages speak of baptism being 'in the name of Jesus' (see, for example, Acts 2.38), which suggests that his name was invoked in some way during the ceremony. This could have been in the form of a statement made over the candidate (e.g., 'I baptize you in the name of . . .'), such as we find in later Syrian usage, but it need not necessarily have been restricted to that. It could also have referred to some confession of faith in Jesus made by the candidate at the moment of baptism, such as we find in later Western sources. At the very least, it seems probable that some sort of ritual dialogue would have preceded the immersion. Acts 2.38 refers to the necessity for repentance to accompany baptism, and this would surely have needed to be expressed verbally. Similarly, Acts 8.37, although found only in certain manuscripts of the text, seems to embody the sort of profession of faith that candidates in some places would have made prior to baptism: 'I believe that Jesus Christ is the Son of God.'

'Confirmation' in the New Testament?
Some scholars have argued that in New Testament times the immersion in water was regularly followed within the same

ceremony by a separate ritual gesture expressing the gift of the Holy Spirit, either in the form of the imposition of hands on the newly baptized or by an anointing with oil, and that this constitutes the biblical foundation of the later practice of 'confirmation'. They point to such passages as Matt. 3.16, Mark 1.10, and Luke 3.22, where Jesus receives the Holy Spirit immediately after his baptism; to Acts 8.14-17, where Peter and John lay their hands on the Samaritans baptized by Philip and they receive the Holy Spirit; to Acts 19.1-7, where baptism is followed by the imposition of Paul's hands and the reception of the Holy Spirit; to Heb. 6.2, which mentions 'the laying on of hands' directly after 'ablutions'; to 2 Cor. 1.22, Eph. 1.13 & 4.30, where Christians are spoken of as having been sealed with the Holy Spirit; to Rev. 7.3, which speaks of the servants of God being sealed upon their foreheads; and to 1 John 2.20 & 27, which refer to an anointing by the Holy One that the readers have received.

Other scholars, however, have contested this interpretation of the passages. They argue that the descriptions of Jesus' baptism do not necessarily mirror the ritual structure of early Christian baptisms, and the two narratives in Acts may not describe the regular form of Christian initiation but instead be accounts of unusual situations: the mission of the Hellenists in Samaria had to be endorsed by the Jerusalem apostles, and the disciples of John needed baptism in the name of Jesus in order to receive the gift of the Holy Spirit.[1] We need to remember that Acts also describes the gift of the Spirit as preceding the act of immersion in the case of the baptism of the household of Cornelius (Acts 10.44-8). Since this episode is usually interpreted as being an exceptional situation, symbolizing a Gentile equivalent of the Pentecost experience (Acts 2.1-4), rather than a description of standard initiatory practice, why should the same not be true of the other baptismal accounts?

As for the other New Testament references cited above, that in Hebrews is too vague to allow any firm conclusions to be drawn about baptismal practice, and the various allusions to 'sealing' and 'anointing' may not be reflections of actual liturgical ceremonies but instead merely vivid metaphors for what was thought to have happened inwardly to those who became Christians.

[1] See Geoffrey Lampe, *The Seal of the Spirit*, 2nd edn (SPCK, London 1967), pp. 64ff.; Gerd Lüdemann, *Early Christianity according to the Traditions in Acts* (Fortress Press, Minneapolis 1989), pp. 96-7, 210-11.

Thus, at best, the New Testament evidence is inconclusive with regard to any post-baptismal ceremonies. Moreover, the theory that the imposition of hands was a standard element in first-century practice becomes still less credible when we take into account the testimony of the later liturgical tradition. As we shall see in subsequent chapters, while North African and Roman sources certainly do seem to have known a post-baptismal anointing and imposition of hands, the early Syrian practice apparently did not include any post-baptismal ceremonies at all, although it was familiar with a pre-baptismal anointing. This later diversity suggests that the whole idea of the existence of a uniform baptismal ritual in primitive Christianity is misconceived. While it is possible that some communities may have practised an anointing and/or imposition of hands from early times, it does not look as if all followed that custom, still less that there was some apostolic directive so to do—or else we would be at a loss to explain the subsequent Syrian departure from that norm.

We cannot even say with total certainty that immersion in water was the one universal element in Christian initiation rites from the beginning. Again, it is possible that immersion was originally limited only to certain groups, with others perhaps having different practices, some of which—such as anointing or foot washing—may have survived as ancillary rites to water baptism in the more standardized initiation process of later centuries.

Baptismal images and metaphors

The language and images used about baptism by the New Testament writers further support the idea that there were variations in liturgical practice from place to place. For what we find here is not a standardized baptismal theology shared by all Christians but a range of different ways of interpreting and expressing what was thought to happen when a person became a Christian. Hebrews 6.4 & 10.32, for instance, speaks of the baptized as having been 'enlightened'. The same image underlies the statement in 1 Peter 2.9 that God has 'called you out of darkness into his marvellous light'; and it recurs, as we shall see in a later chapter, in the description of baptism in the second-century writer Justin Martyr. John 3, on the other hand, uses instead the metaphor of rebirth by water and Spirit; a similar concept also appears in Titus 3.5, which speaks of 'the washing of regeneration and renewal in the Holy Spirit'; and once again this idea is picked up by Justin Martyr. In the Acts of the Apostles, the emphasis falls instead on the forgiveness of sins and the gift of the Holy Spirit, as, for example, in Acts 2.38: 'And Peter said to them, "Repent, and be baptized every one of you in the name of Jesus Christ for the forgiveness of your sins; and you shall receive the gift of the Holy Spirit."'

By contrast to these ways of speaking, in Paul's baptismal theology the primary image seems to have been union with Christ through participation in his death and resurrection (see especially Rom. 6.2ff.; Col. 2.12). But he also makes use of other metaphors. As we have mentioned earlier, he speaks of Christians as having been sealed as God's people: '[God] has put his seal upon us and given us his Spirit in our hearts as a guarantee' (2 Cor. 1.22). The same image recurs in the Epistle to the Ephesians, where the readers are said to have been 'sealed with the promised Holy Spirit, which is the guarantee of our inheritance . . .' (1.13–14; see also 4.30); and a similar theme is found in Rev. 7.30, which speaks of the servants of God being sealed upon their foreheads. This metaphor seems to be derived from commerce, where a seal authenticated a change of ownership: Christians were once slaves to sin, but now they have been marked as belonging instead to God (see Rom. 6.16–23), and the Holy Spirit constitutes, as it were, the 'deposit' which guarantees that the transaction will brought to completion when Christ returns.

Gal. 3.27 offers what seems to be yet another metaphorical image, that of baptism as being clothed in a new garment, since it describes the baptized as having 'put on Christ'; and Col. 3.9–10 and Eph. 4.22–4 speak of putting off the old nature and putting on the new. There is also a similar eschatological picture in 2 Cor. 5.1–5, which talks of the longing 'to put on our heavenly dwelling, so that . . . we may not be found naked.' Such language may well have arisen as result of baptismal candidates stripping off their clothes and going down naked into the water and then dressing again when they emerged from it. Although we have no first-century testimony that this was then the usual practice, it is well attested in later sources. To these citations, we may perhaps add the references in Mark's Gospel to the young man at the arrest of Jesus who left the linen cloth he was wearing and ran away naked (14.51–2) and of the young man sitting on the right side of the empty tomb, dressed in a white robe (16.5). Robin Scroggs and Kent Goff have suggested that this pair of stories was intended as a baptismal image,[2] and this is certainly an attractive interpretation of passages which have often puzzled commentators. It is interesting to observe that fourth-century sources speak of the newly-baptized not just putting back on their former garments, but being clothed in white robes. Could this practice possibly go back to New Testament times, or is it—as seems more likely—a much later development that was encouraged by such texts as Rev. 7.9–14, which describes the countless multitude wearing robes washed white in the blood of the Lamb?

Finally, we should note that the image of being 'anointed' with the Holy Spirit found in 1 John 2.20 & 27 arose out of a different concept from that of being 'sealed' with the Spirit used in the Pauline writings. In Israelite tradition both kings and priests had been anointed when they were appointed, as a sign that they had been chosen by God. For example, in 1 Sam. 16.1–13 the prophet Samuel anoints David as king 'and the Spirit of the Lord came mightily upon David from that day forward'. The term 'Messiah' itself means in Hebrew 'the anointed one', which was translated into Greek as *Christos*, Christ; and so it is hardly surprising that early Christian writers thought of Jesus as having been anointed by God with the Holy Spirit (see Luke 4.16; Acts 4.27; Acts 10.38) or at least as having received God's spirit at his baptism (Matt. 3.16; Mark 1.10; Luke 3.22). Since they believed that Christians at their baptism received the same Holy Spirit, it was but a small step to think that they, too, were being anointed as Jesus had been. The idea that Christians constituted a 'royal priesthood' (1 Peter 2.9; see also 2.5) or a 'kingdom of priests' (Rev. 1.6; see also 5.10), which was derived from Exod. 19.6, would also have contributed to seeing baptism as anointing. Both these images led quite naturally to the adoption of a literal anointing with oil as a baptismal ceremony, such as we find in later sources.

FOR FURTHER READING:

G. R. Beasley-Murray, *Baptism in the New Testament* (Macmillan, London 1962).

Adela Yarbro Collins, 'The Origin of Christian Baptism', *Studia Liturgica* 19 (1989), pp. 28-46.

Oscar Cullmann, *Baptism in the New Testament* (SCM Press, London 1950).

W. F. Flemington, *The New Testament Doctrine of Baptism* (SPCK, London 1964).

---

[2] Robin Scroggs & Kent I. Goff, 'Baptism in Mark: Dying and Rising with Christ', *Journal of Biblical Literature* 92 (1973), pp. 531-48.

2. Syria and Egypt

SYRIA

Our sources of information for baptismal practice in the early Syrian tradition are rather sparse, but enough to enable us to piece together a rough outline of how Christian initiation was performed and understood there in the second and third centuries.

The Didache

Chapter 7 of the ancient church order known as the *Didache*, or 'Teaching of the Twelve Apostles', paints a very simple picture:

> Concerning baptism, baptize thus: having first recounted all these things, baptize in the name of the Father and of the Son and of the Holy Spirit in living water; if you do not have living water, baptize in other water; if you cannot in cold, then in warm; if you do not have either, pour water three times on the head in the name of Father, Son, and Holy Spirit. Before the baptism let the baptizer and the one to be baptized and any others who are able first fast; you shall instruct the one to be baptized to fast one or two [days] before.

Scholars have found it difficult to date the *Didache* precisely, but usually place its compilation somewhere between the second half of the first century and the first half of the second century. These instructions suggest that the normal pattern of Christian initiation consisted of a period of instruction and fasting, by both candidate and at least some members of the Christian community, followed by immersion in running water accompanied by the recitation of the name of the Trinity. The scholar Arthur Vööbus, however, believes that this trinitarian formula is a later addition to the text, and that the original version was simply baptism in the name of the Lord.[1] Nevertheless, the formula is reminiscent of Matt. 28.19–20 ('Go therefore and make disciples of all nations, baptizing them in the name of the Father and of the Son and of the Holy Spirit, teaching them to observe all I have commanded you . . .'); and whenever they were written, both passages imply that the earliest custom of invoking the name of Jesus in baptism was

---

[1] *Liturgical Traditions in the Didache* (ETSE, Stockholm 1968), pp. 35–9. There is also a passage in the apocryphal *Acts of Paul* where Thecla immerses herself in water, saying 'In the name of Jesus Christ I baptize myself . . .', which seems to point to a formula something like 'I baptize you in the name of Jesus Christ' as having been usual in early times. See J. K. Elliot, *The Apocryphal New Testament* (Clarendon, Oxford 1993), p. 370.

eventually expanded in this way, as the Church began to define its faith more fully. Other sources confirm that what was intended by these references was that the one baptizing should say over the candidate: 'I baptize you in the name of the Father and of the Son and of the Holy Spirit.'

The main concern of the baptismal instructions in the *Didache*, however, is to make provision for occasions when it was impossible to perform the ritual in what was seen as the normal way: immersion in cold, running water. Again, this suggests the Church was undergoing a transition from an outdoor, missionary context to a more domestic situation that required some modification of its earlier practices.

The Didascalia

When we compare these simple directions with other early Syrian sources, however, the most striking feature is the important place that the others give to a pre-baptismal anointing with oil. The third-century Syrian church order known as the *Didascalia Apostolorum*, for example, requires female deacons to be appointed in order to carry out this ministry for women candidates, and it instructs the bishop as follows:

> In the first place, when women go down into the baptismal water: those who go down into the water ought to be anointed by a deaconess with the oil of anointing; and where there is no woman to hand, and especially no deaconess, he who baptizes must of necessity anoint the woman who is being baptized. But where there is a woman, and especially a deaconess, present, it is not fitting that women should be seen by men, but with the imposition of the hand you should anoint the head only. As of old priests and kings were anointed in Israel, so do you likewise, with the imposition of the hand, anoint the head of those who receive baptism, whether it be of men or of women; and afterwards, whether you yourself baptize, or you tell the deacons or presbyters to baptize, let a woman, a deaconess, anoint the women, as we have already said. But let a man pronounce over them the invocation of the divine names in the water.[2]

It is clear that the *Didascalia* regards the unction of the candidates' heads performed by the bishop as an expression of their entry into the royal priesthood of the Church (see 1 Peter 2.5 & 9; Rev. 1.6; 5.10). But it also seems that it was expected that

[2] *Didascalia* 3.12; English translation from Sebastian Brock & Michael Vasey, *The Liturgical Portions of the Didascalia* (Grove Books, Nottingham 1982), p. 22.

their whole bodies would be anointed as well: otherwise, there would have been no necessity for the female deacons.

The Acts of Thomas

We come across this same twofold unction in other Syrian texts from the same period. The third-century apocryphal *Acts of Thomas* contains several descriptions of baptisms. Two refer to an anointing of the head alone before the immersion and associate this with the Messiah (chs. 27 & 132). Two others include a prayer for the blessing of the oil, mention the anointing of both the head and the whole body, and associate the action instead with healing (chs. 121 & 157). A fifth account speaks explicitly only of the immersion in water, at least in the Syriac version of the text, although an allusion to the 'seal' here could be an oblique reference to anointing (ch. 49).

While it is possible to harmonize these various accounts of anointing by surmising that an unction of both head and body was presumed in every case, but only explicitly mentioned in two of them, the scholar Gabriele Winkler has put forward the theory that they represent two different stages of development in the baptismal rite: the earlier practice was to anoint the head alone, as continued to be the custom in the later Armenian rite, and the anointing of the whole body was a later addition to the ritual. She argues that, in the earliest tradition:

> Christian baptism is shaped after Christ's baptism in the Jordan. As Jesus had received the anointing through the divine presence in the appearance of a dove, and was invested as the Messiah, so in Christian baptism every candidate is anointed and, in connection with this anointing, the gift of the Spirit is conferred. Therefore the main theme of this prebaptismal anointing is the entry into the eschatological kingship of the Messiah, being in the true sense of the word assimilated to the Messiah-King through this anointing.[3]

Winkler believes that this explains why at first oil was poured over the head alone (this was the custom at the anointing of the kings of Israel), why the coming of the Spirit was associated with it (the Spirit of the Lord came over the newly nominated king), and why it was the anointing and not the immersion in water that seemed to be regarded as the central feature of baptism in the early Syrian sources (this was the only visible gesture for what was held

[3] 'The Original Meaning of the Prebaptismal Anointing and its Implications', *Worship* 52 (1978), p. 36.

to be the central event at Christ's baptism—his revelation as the Messiah-King through the descent of the Spirit). The later introduction of the anointing of the whole body would thus have led to a reinterpretation of the significance of the oil in terms of a healing of the whole person, and hence to the addition of prayers that sanctified the oil and invested it with healing power.

Of course, it is equally possible that what we have here may be not so much a later addition to the earlier rite as the beginning of a fusion into a more composite form of what had originally been separate traditions. While some early Christian communities in Syria may have done as Winkler suggests and adopted an anointing of the head as a symbol of participation in the spirit of the Messiah, others may have practised instead an anointing of the whole body as a symbol of protection and healing, perhaps influenced by pagan religions; others who included an unction of the head may have related it directly to the Old Testament custom of anointing kings and priests (as is the case in the *Didascalia*) rather than to Jesus' anointing with the Spirit at his baptism; and still other groups may have known only a simple immersion in water, as seems to be the case in the *Didache*. It is even possible that at least some of those for whom the anointing was the central feature of initiation may not at first have included a water baptism at all in their practice. Thus, only gradually would these Syrian Christians have appropriated elements and concepts from one another's traditions into their own. This might help to explain why the anointing with the Spirit precedes rather than follows the water bath, in contrast to the sequence of the gospel accounts of Jesus' own baptism.

Faith and baptism

The Syrian sources also reveal another distinctive feature in their initiation practice, a two-stage ritual. The *Didascalia* offers the first sign of this in its statement that 'when the heathen desire and promise to repent, saying "We believe", we receive them into the congregation so that they may hear the word, but do not receive them into communion until they receive the seal and are fully initiated'.[4] It may seem odd that converts were expected to express their repentance and faith *before* they were allowed to hear the word, but probably what is meant here is that, while there would have been some preliminary instruction designed to bring them to

[4] 2.39 (Brock & Vasey, *The Liturgical Portions of the Didascalia*, p. 12).

repentance and faith, certain teachings were reserved until after they had made an expression of commitment to Christ. Although the teaching had apparently disappeared from this interval by the fourth century, John Chrysostom seems to have known at Antioch both a formula of renunciation of evil and an act of adherence to Christ ('I pledge myself to you, O Christ') still occurring on the day before the baptism. A similar pattern can also be found in the rite of Constantinople in the fifth century; and the testimony of Theodore of Mopsuestia (fourth century) and of the later Syrian rites show traces of this twofold structure, even though both parts now take place on the same occasion.

Conclusions

If we can generalize at all from this early Syrian evidence—and that may be a dangerous thing to do—we could perhaps describe the understanding of initiation here as being primarily *Christological* in character. The act of commitment to Christ seems to mark the key turning-point in the process, and what followed after articulated ritually the positive consequences of that act: the candidate was admitted to receive Christ's teaching, anointed with the priestly/kingly/messianic spirit which Christ had received at his baptism in the Jordan, and immersed in the water in the name of the Lord (later of the Trinity). Because the gospel accounts of Jesus' baptism link it with the affirmation of Christ's divine sonship ('You are my beloved Son'), fourth-century Syrian writers also portray Christian baptism as a birth to new life, and speak of the baptismal font both as the Jordan and as a womb.

EGYPT

The complete pattern of the earliest baptismal practice in Egypt is not easy to discern because of a lack of evidence, but certain features can be made out. In some respects there are resemblances to Syrian practice. In particular, like the Syrian rites, the Egyptian tradition seems at first to have known only a pre-baptismal anointing and no post-baptismal ceremonies. The meaning attached to this anointing is not very fully spelled out, but it is clearly considered integral to the baptism, is certainly not exorcistic in character, and appears to have been accompanied by a trinitarian formula, which we also find in fourth-century Syrian sources. A prayer over the oil in the fourth-century *Sacramentary of Sarapion* speaks of its function in terms of healing and re-creation; Cyril of

Alexandria (*d.* 444) termed it the 'chrism of catechesis'; and the later Coptic rites call it 'the oil of gladness'—a designation also used by John Chrysostom in Antioch. On the other hand, in at least two respects Egyptian practice was different from the Syrian.

The baptismal season

As in other parts of the world, baptism was usually preceded by a period of fasting by both candidates and community. As it had become the custom in Egypt from early times—we do not know exactly when—for Christians to observe a forty-day season of fasting in imitation of Jesus' fast in the wilderness immediately after their celebration of his baptism on January 6 (see below, p. 89), the end of this fast was adopted as the preferred time of year for Christian baptisms to take place, and the forty days then constituted the period of the catechumenate. The candidates were apparently enrolled as catechumens at the beginning of that season, received instruction and fasted together with the Christian community during it, and underwent a final scrutiny as to their readiness for admission to baptism two days before the end of it and the time for the administration of the baptismal rite.

The profession of faith

In another respect, Egyptian baptismal practice seems to have resembled Western rather than Eastern custom. It appears from third-century sources that the immersion in water was accompanied or preceded by credal interrogation similar to that found in North Africa and at Rome (in which the candidates responded to questions about their belief in the Trinity—see below, pp. 18–19), rather than by an affirmation of faith of the kind revealed in Syrian sources, where prior to the baptismal event the candidates themselves made a statement professing their adherence to Christ. However, there are some signs that the fivefold confession of faith found instead of this in later Coptic liturgical rites may have also existed in early times, perhaps as an alternative to the interrogatory form in some places.

FOR FURTHER READING:

Paul F. Bradshaw (ed.), *Essays in Early Eastern Initiation* (Grove Books, Nottingham 1988).

Gabriele Winkler, 'The History of the Syriac Prebaptismal Anointing in the Light of the Earliest Armenian Sources', in *Symposium Syriacum 1976*, Orientalia Christiana Analecta 205 (Rome 1978), pp. 317–24.

3. Rome and North Africa

Justin Martyr

Our earliest evidence comes from Justin Martyr, writing in the middle of the second century. He describes baptism thus:

> As many as are persuaded and believe that these things which we describe and teach are true, and undertake to live accordingly, are taught to pray and ask God, while fasting, for the forgiveness of their sins; and we pray and fast with them. Then they are led by us to a place where there is water, and they are reborn after the manner of rebirth by which we also were reborn: for they are then washed in the water in the name of the Father and Lord God of all things, and of our Saviour Jesus Christ, and of the Holy Spirit . . .
>
> . . . over him that now chooses to be reborn and repents of his sins is named the Father and Lord God of all things. This name only is called upon by him that leads to the washing him that is to be washed: for no one can speak the Name of God, who is ineffable; and anyone who might boldly claim to do so is quite mad. This washing is called enlightenment, because those who are experiencing these things have their minds enlightened. And he that is being enlightened is washed in the Name of Jesus Christ who was crucified under Pontius Pilate, and in the name of the Holy Spirit, which through the prophets foretold all things concerning Jesus.
>
> After we have thus washed him that is persuaded and declares his assent, we lead him to those who are called brethren, where they are assembled, and make common prayer fervently for ourselves, for him that has been enlightened, and for all men everywhere. . . . When we have ended the prayers, we greet one another with a kiss. Then bread and a cup of water and of mixed wine are brought to him that presides over the brethren. . . .[1]

The process thus appears relatively simple, consisting of a period (of unspecified duration) of instruction, fasting, and prayer, by both candidate and community before the baptism; then immersion itself, accompanied in some way by the assent of the candidate and the naming of the Trinity; and finally the entry into the assembly of other Christians to share in common prayer, the kiss, and the celebration of the eucharist with them. Apart from the absence of any reference to an anointing, therefore, this description sounds very similar to what we have seen in Syria.

On the other hand, it is necessary to remember that Justin Martyr was here writing a defence of Christianity to the Emperor Antoninus Pius, and so may not have included full details of everything that went on, nor indeed have been referring specifically to

---

[1] *I Apol.* 61, 65; English translation from *DBL*, p. 2 (with minor additions).

practice at Rome but instead providing a generic outline of Christian baptismal customs. A small number of scholars have tried to argue that if one reads between the lines of Justin's writings. it is possible to discern there evidence suggesting that Justin did not regard water baptism as the whole of Christian initiation, but also knew of a post-baptismal ceremony that effected the gift of the Holy Spirit.[2] Their arguments have, however, failed to convince many.[3]

It is interesting to note the images used by Justin to describe the meaning of the ritual: the New Testament ideas of rebirth, washing, and enlightenment predominate; but there is no hint of the Pauline notion of participation in the death and resurrection of Christ. One might easily suppose that Justin omitted this simply because it would not have been easily intelligible to a pagan audience, but in fact hardly any Christian writer before the fourth century draws on that Pauline concept in connection with baptism. Hence, it seems as if it was not yet used as the central interpretation of the meaning of baptism that it was to become in later times.

The Apostolic Tradition

Many scholars would add to the apparent Roman evidence provided by Justin Martyr the baptismal instructions contained in an enigmatic church order, usually identified as being the *Apostolic Tradition* written by Hippolytus of Rome in the early third century. However, some scholars believe that this attribution may be mistaken, and so the church order may not reflect Roman practice, nor may it contents necessarily date from the early third century. Instead, it could well be a composite document made up of a number of different elements originating in different time periods, some perhaps as old as the second century, others no older than the early fourth century. For this reason, we shall not

---

[2] See especially Gregory Dix, '"The Seal" in the Second Century', *Theology* 51 (1948), pp. 7–12; E. C. Ratcliff, 'Justin Martyr and Confirmation', *Theology* 51 (1948), pp. 133–9 = A. H. Couratin & David Tripp (eds.), *E. C. Ratcliff. Liturgical Studies* (SPCK, London 1976), pp. 110–17; A. H. Couratin, 'Justin Martyr and Confirmation—A Note', *Theology* 55 (1952), pp. 458–60; L. S. Thornton, *Confirmation: Its Place in the Baptismal Mystery* (SPCK, London 1954), pp. 34–51. See also J. D. C. Fisher, *Confirmation Then and Now* (SPCK, London 1978), pp. 11–21.

[3] See, for example, Lampe, *The Seal of the Spirit*, pp. 109–11; L. L. Mitchell, *Baptismal Anointing* (SPCK, London 1966), pp. 13–15.

use it here to try to establish what baptismal customs might have been at Rome in the century after Justin Martyr. But since some—though by no means all—of what it prescribes is similar to what we learn from our principal North African witness from this period, Tertullian, we shall note those parallels as we examine his testimony.

NORTH AFRICA

Tertullian, writing around the beginning of the third century, does not offer a single continuous account of the baptismal ritual, but from the various references to it that are scattered throughout his writings, we can reconstruct the process known to him as follows:[4]

The preferred baptismal season

> The Passover [Easter] provides the day of most solemnity for baptism, for then was accomplished our Lord's passion, and into it we are baptized. . . . After that, Pentecost is a most auspicious period for arranging baptisms, for during it our Lord's resurrection was several times made known among the disciples, and the grace of the Holy Spirit first given. . . . For all that, every day is a Lord's day: any hour, any season is suitable for baptism (*De baptismo* 19).

This was not just an idiosyncratic idea of Tertullian's, for we find the same preference for Easter expressed in one of the genuine writings of Hippolytus of Rome, and a possible hint of it in the *Apostolic Tradition*.[5] This suggests that in North Africa and at Rome there were the beginnings of a recovery of Paul's theology of baptism as participation in the death and resurrection of Christ.

Preparation

> Those who are at the point of entering upon baptism ought to pray, with frequent prayers, fastings, bendings of the knee, and all-night vigils, along with the confession of all their sins, so as to make a copy of the baptism of John (*De baptismo* 20).

Like the Syrian sources, Tertullian does not indicate whether there was a formally structured catechumenate lasting for an extended length of time, but there was no doubt some period of instruction, and this quotation implies the existence of a final stage of preparation that was particularly expressive of repentance.

---

[4] All texts cited are taken from *DBL*, pp. 7–10.
[5] Hippolytus, *Commentary on Daniel* 13.15; *AT* 20 (p. 17).

Vestiges of older practices in a number of later sources from various parts of the world suggest that at one time this final stage lasted for three weeks,[6] which may well have been the custom known to Tertullian.

Apostolic Tradition 15–20, on the other hand, contains much more extensive directions for the period of preparation, including the expectation that the catechumenate will normally last three years, a list of occupations deemed incompatible with being a Christian (most of which can be paralleled in Tertullian's works), the careful examination of the conduct of the candidates during their catechumenate to ensure that a real change in their way of life had taken place, and frequent exorcism during the final stage before baptism. Some of this material may originate from a later period than that of Tertullian, or to a region of the world where the catechumenal process had developed further by this time.

Prayer over the water

> All waters, when God is invoked, acquire the sacred significance of conveying sanctity: for at once the Spirit comes down from heaven and stays upon the waters, sanctifying them from within himself, and when thus sanctified they absorb the power of sanctifying. . . . Thus when the waters have in some sense acquired healing power by an angel's intervention, the spirit is in those waters corporally washed, while the flesh is in those same waters spiritually cleansed.(*De baptismo* 4).

Tertullian is the very first person to mention the invocation of the Holy Spirit over the water, and it probably arose as a result of the change in the location of baptisms, from rivers and lakes to indoor baths or tanks, to which we earlier saw the *Didache* allude. While the naturally flowing character of the former could enable them to be seen as 'living' and already imbued with God's spirit, the water in the latter would have seemed deficient in this respect, and hence in need of investing with the power that they lacked.[7] We have already seen this happening with regard to the oil used in Syria, and it is interesting to note that Tertullian describes the power bestowed on the sanctified water as that of healing, as is also the case with Syrian oil.

[6] See Maxwell Johnson, 'From Three Weeks to Forty Days: Baptismal Preparation and the Origins of Lent', *Studia Liturgica* 20 (1990), pp. 185–200.

[7] See J. D. C. Fisher, 'The Consecration of Water in the Early Rites of Baptism', *Studia Patristica* 2 (1957), pp. 41–6.

18

The renunciation of evil

When on the point of coming to the water we then and there, as also somewhat earlier in church under the bishop's control, affirm that we renounce the devil and his pomp and his angels (*De corona* 3).

Tertullian's description suggests that the renunciation happened more than once during the period of preparation for baptism as well as immediately before the immersion. Elsewhere he speaks of renouncing 'the devil, his retinue, and his works'.[8] It may have been in the form of a direct address to the devil by the candidate, such as is attested in the *Apostolic Tradition*, 'I renounce you, Satan, and all your service and all your works'; or it may have been in the form of a response to a question put to the candidate ('Do you renounce . . .'), such as we find in later sources, often divided into a three parts (Satan, works, pomps), in order to parallel the threefold profession of faith.[9]

The triple profession of faith and triple immersion

When we have entered the water, we make profession of the Christian faith in the words of its rule (*De spectaculis* 4).

We are thrice immersed, while we answer interrogations rather more extensive than our Lord has prescribed in the gospel (*De corona* 3).

For not once only, but thrice are we baptized into each of the three persons at each of the several names (*Adversus Praxean* 26).

The flesh is washed that the soul may be made spotless (*De resurrectione carnis* 8).

Tertullian's brief references do not supply a very clear picture of the practice, but we can fill out what is probably in mind by means of the more detailed directions in the *Apostolic Tradition*. Although its text is not entirely clear at this particular point, it appears that the original directed:

As he who is to be baptized is descending into the water, let him who baptizes him say thus: 'Do you believe in God the Father omnipotent?' And let the one being baptized say, 'I believe.' And the giver, having his hand placed on his head, shall baptize him once. And then he shall say: 'Do you believe in Christ Jesus, the Son of God, who was born from the Holy Spirit from the Virgin Mary, and was crucified under Pontius Pilate, and died, and

[8] *De spectaculis* 4 (*DBL*, p. 9).

[9] See *DBL*, p. 183, for the later Roman form. At Milan, at least from the time of Ambrose onwards, the question was in two parts (devil and his works; the world and its pleasures—later, his world and his pomps): ibid., pp. 128, 131, 137, 143, 148.

rose again on the third day alive from the dead, and ascended into heaven, and sits on the right hand of the Father, and will come to judge the living and the dead?' And when he has said, 'I believe', he shall be baptized again. And he shall say again: 'Do you believe in the Holy Spirit and the holy Church and the resurrection of the flesh? Then he who is being baptized shall say, 'I believe', and thus he shall be baptized a third time.[10]

The particular formulation of the statement of belief known to Tertullian may not have developed quite as fully as this one, but one can easily see that it was out of baptismal professions of faith of this kind that the so-called Apostles' Creed evolved;[11] and it was doubtless the transition from a simple declaration of faith in Jesus to a trinitarian affirmation that caused the immersion also to assume a triple character.

This element constitutes one of the most striking differences from Syrian practice. While in Syria the candidates' expression of belief had taken place before they approached the water, and the immersion was accompanied by a trinitarian formula spoken over the candidate, here the trinitarian profession of faith itself in effect constitutes the baptismal formula. It thus offered a vivid visual representation of the intimate connection that was understood to exist between faith and baptism. For there was no suggestion for Tertullian or other early Christian theologians that baptism could somehow 'work' without the presence of faith in the candidate. Tertullian himself affirmed that 'that washing is a sealing of faith, which faith is begun and is commended by the faith of repentance. We are not washed in order that we may cease sinning, but because we have ceased, since in heart we have been bathed already' (*De penitentia* 6). Similarly, Origen in Alexandria maintained that 'if someone who is still sinning comes to the bath, he does not receive the forgiveness of sins' (*Hom. in Luc.* 21). Naturally, the requirement of faith presented something of a problem in the case of infant baptism, as we shall see in a later chapter.

Post-baptismal anointing

After that we come up from the washing and are anointed with the blessed unction, following that ancient practice by which, ever since Aaron was

[10] *AT* 21 (p. 19). The first two sentences, however, have been reconstructed on the basis of the version of the document found in the later church order known as the *Testamentum Domini*.

[11] See J. N. D. Kelly, *Early Christian Creeds* (Longmans, Green, & Co., London 1950), pp. 30ff.

anointed by Moses, there was a custom of anointing them for priesthood with oil out of a horn. That is why [the high priest] is called a christ, from 'chrism' which is [the Greek for] 'anointing'; and from this also our Lord obtained his title, though it had become a spiritual anointing, in that he was anointed with the Spirit of God the Father (*De baptismo* 7).

The flesh is anointed that the soul may be consecrated (*De resurrectione carnis* 8).

Here we encounter a close parallel to the anointing and its interpretation found in the Syrian *Didascalia*—but in a quite different position, following rather than preceding the immersion.

Sign of the cross

The flesh is signed [with the cross] that the soul too may be protected (*De resurrectione carnis* 8).

Tertullian apparently understands this post-baptismal ceremony to have a protective function, God's mark on a person being able to ward off evil powers.

Imposition of hands with prayer

Next follows the imposition of the hand in benediction, inviting and welcoming the Holy Spirit (*De baptismo* 8).

The flesh is overshadowed by the imposition of the hand that the soul may be illumined by the Spirit (*De resurrectione carnis* 8).

Here is another major difference from Syrian practice, not merely in the presence of a post-baptismal imposition of hands, but in Tertullian's association of that particular gesture with the gift of the Holy Spirit. There is a similar imposition of hands with prayer in *Apostolic Tradition* 21, and some versions of the text of that prayer associate the action with the bestowal of the Spirit, while others speak of the baptized having already received the Spirit through their immersion in the water.

Eucharist, including milk and honey

Made welcome then [into the assembly] we partake of a compound of milk and honey (*De corona* 3).

The flesh feeds on the body and blood of Christ so that the soul as well may be replete with God (*De resurrectione carnis* 8).

The same custom, of offering the newly baptized milk and honey together with the bread and wine in the celebration of the eucharist that concluded their initiation rite, is also attested in

Apostolic Tradition 21, which explicitly relates its symbolism to the fulfilment of the Old Testament promise that God's people would inherit a land flowing with milk and honey.

Conclusion

All this is very different in a number of respects from what we encountered in Syria. In contrast to the *Christological* character that we ascribed to initiation there, this might perhaps be described as *soteriological*: the biblical model is not Christ's baptism in the Jordan, but rather his passage from death to resurrection, in which the candidates symbolically share, by renouncing this evil world and going down into the water, where they proclaim their faith and come up again to be anointed as God's priestly people, to be marked as his own with the sign of the cross, to receive the Spirit of the risen Lord, and to enter the promised land.

4. The Fourth-Century Synthesis

The cessation of persecution against the Church in the early fourth century brought a major change in the practice of Christian initiation. Because it was now safe and respectable to become a Christian, there was a considerable increase in the number of people wanting to join the Church. However, not all of these took the step because they had experienced an inner conversion: some did so from less worthy motives, such as the desire to marry a Christian or to please a master or friend, or because it promised to be advantageous to their career or political ambitions. Moreover, once having become catechumens, many people were in no hurry to complete the process of initiation. Since they were already regarded as Christians, they saw no need to proceed to baptism itself, especially as that would leave no second chance to obtain the forgiveness of sins that baptism was believed to convey: it seemed preferable to delay the actual baptism as long as possible so as to be sure of having all one's sins forgiven and so of gaining salvation. Consequently, many parents enrolled their children as catechumens early in their life but delayed presenting them for baptism at least until after the passions of youth had subsided and there was less chance of them succumbing to temptation; and many adults deferred their own baptism until they became seriously ill and feared that they might die unbaptized.

All of this had a profound effect on the nature of the baptismal process itself. Whereas in primitive Christianity it had functioned as a ritual expression of a genuine conversion experience that candidates were already undergoing in their lives, now in the fourth century the baptismal process became instead the means of conveying a profound experience to the candidates in the hope of bringing about their conversion. In order to accomplish this new role, the process became much more dramatic—one might even say theatrical—in character. Taking their cue from contemporary pagan mystery religions, the ceremonies surrounding baptism became highly elaborate and cloaked in such great secrecy that candidates would have no idea in advance what was going to happen to them, with the aim of producing a powerful emotional and psychological impression upon them. Only after they had experienced the celebration of baptism and the eucharist was an explanation of the meaning of the sacred mysteries in which they had partaken then given to them in what was called mystagogy—post-baptismal instruction, usually during the week following their initiation.

The frequent lack of obvious signs of conversion in the behaviour of the newly baptized also had a significant impact on baptismal theology in another way. On the one hand, fourth-century preachers continued to insist on the need for real faith and amendment of life if baptism was to be efficacious, just as their predecessors in the third century had done, and engaged in substantial pre-baptismal instruction in order to impress upon the candidates the great importance of the step that they were taking. On the other hand, there was at the same time a growing tendency in theological discussion to focus on the invisible transformation that was believed to take place in baptism rather than to look for visible changes in the conduct of the newly baptized. For example, theologians increasingly understood the term 'seal' from the New Testament not as a vivid metaphor but as a metaphysical reality: as the invisible imprint of the divine image upon the human soul.[1]

Another major characteristic of Christian initiation in the fourth century was a tendency for the varied baptismal practices in the different regions of early Christianity to coalesce into a more homogeneous pattern. The primary sources of our information about this are the baptismal homilies delivered by four leading bishops of the period: in the West, Ambrose of Milan; in the East, John Chrysostom (at Antioch), Cyril of Jerusalem, and Theodore of Mopsuestia.[2] The table on the next page gives a schematic view of their evidence. Not surprisingly, Jerusalem (to which pilgrims were now flocking from both East and West) appears to have been the first Eastern centre of Christianity to incorporate into its liturgical practice certain elements that were similar to Western customs.

The baptismal season

The choice of a preferred season for baptisms serves as a good example of this development. As we have seen, in Egypt the conclusion of the forty-day post-Epiphany fast was the normal occasion for the celebration of baptism, and Rome and North Africa had a preference for Easter, while the Syrian tradition does not appear to have known of any preferential time. By the middle of the fourth century, however, we find an almost universal custom of Easter as the preferred season for all baptisms, and along with

[1] See Lampe, *The Seal of the Spirit*, esp. pp. 247ff.
[2] English translations in *AIR*.

Ambrose	Cyril	Chrysostom/Theodore
	Renunciation	Renunciation
	Act of adherence	Act of adherence
'Opening'		Anointing of head
Entry to baptistery	Entry to baptistery	(Ch: 'at night')
(Removal of clothes)	Removal of clothes	Removal of clothes
Anointing of body	Anointing of body	Anointing of body
Renunciation		
Blessing of water	(Blessing of water)	Blessing of water
Immersion with profession of faith	Immersion with profession of faith	Immersion with trinitarian formula
Anointing of head	Anointing of head, ears, nose, chest	
Washing of feet		
(White garment)	White garment	White garment
'Sealing'		(Th: seal on forehead) (Ch: kiss)
Eucharist	Eucharist	Eucharist

that—not surprisingly—the gradual adoption of the Pauline theology of baptism as participation in the death and resurrection of Christ. Thus Cyril, while retaining elements of the older baptismal imagery of the Syrian tradition, adds to it the understanding of the whole process as a symbolic imitation of the passion of Christ. He says to the newly baptized:

stripped naked, . . . you were imitating Christ naked upon the cross. . . .
You were conducted by the hand to the holy pool of sacred baptism, just as
Christ was conveyed from the cross to the sepulchre . . . and submerged
yourselves three times in the water and emerged: by this symbolic gesture
you were secretly re-enacting the burial of Christ three days in the tomb.[3]

The catechumenate

We also find that by the second half of the fourth century the
Egyptian custom of a forty-day period of fasting prior to baptism
had been taken up by every other church throughout the world,
creating the season of Lent (see below, pp. 89–90). Those who
wished to be baptized at Easter had their names recorded at the
beginning of the season (after being admitted as catechumens, if
this had not previously happened); and during this time of preparation there occurred not only the instruction and fasting of which
earlier sources had spoken, but also the exorcism of the candidates,
the frequency of which varied from place to place: while in North
Africa it seems to have happened only once, at Rome it occurred
on three successive Sundays, and at Antioch and Jerusalem it was
repeated daily.[4]

Apart from *Apostolic Tradition* 18 (where it is prescribed on a
daily basis), this regular exorcism of all baptismal candidates is
clearly attested for the first time only in fourth-century sources,
but it is probably a much older custom, and has its roots in the
New Testament practice of driving out evil spirits from those
thought to be possessed. At some unknown point in the history of
the Church, this action was extended from particular individuals to
every convert, reflecting the early Christian belief that all pagans
were in the possession of the devil and needed to be liberated in
order to become Christians and receive the Holy Spirit. As a
second-century source affirms, 'before we believed in God, the
dwelling-place of our heart was corrupt and weak . . . because it
was full of idolatry and was the home of demons, since we did
everything that was opposed to God.'[5] The same attitude is
reflected in the prohibition in *Apostolic Tradition* 18 against
catechumens either praying with or exchanging a ritual kiss with
baptized Christians, because they were still impure.

Both *Apostolic Tradition* 18 and Ambrose describe a final
preparatory ceremony in which the bishop touches the ears and

[3] *Mystagogical Catechesis* 2.2,4 (*AIR*, pp. 74, 76).

[4] *DBL*, pp. 102, 108, 166-9; *AIR*, pp. 4-11.

[5] *Epistle of Barnabas* 16.7, cited from *AIR*, p. 6.

noses of the candidates (and the forehead, too, in the *Apostolic Tradition*). In the *Apostolic Tradition* this action follows an exorcism, involves the sign of the cross, and is clearly intended as a 'sealing', to protect the candidates against the return of evil spirits. Ambrose, however, describes it as an 'opening', and interprets it in the light of Jesus' opening of the ears and mouth of man who was deaf and dumb (Mark 7.32–7), but he has some difficulty in explaining why it is the nose and not the mouth that is touched by the bishop, and he has to resort to saying that it is so that candidates may be 'the aroma of Christ to God' (2 Cor. 2.15).[6] It looks as though what was originally an act symbolizing protection has been not very successfully reinterpreted here.

The pre-baptismal anointing

As we can see from the table, both Eastern and Western rites now have a pre-baptismal anointing. We do not know when the practice was introduced in the West. Although it appears in the *Apostolic Tradition*, we cannot be sure how ancient this part of the text is. Its role there is described as exorcistic and it is applied with the words, 'Let every evil spirit depart from you'. Ambrose, however, describes the practice in slightly different terms: he speaks of the candidates being 'rubbed with oil like an athlete, Christ's athlete, as though in preparation for an earthly wrestling-match'.[7] In spite of these differences, both sources agree that it functioned in some way against the power of evil, whether as a protective shield or as preparatory for combat with the devil.

It is to be noted that what is being described in both cases is an anointing of the whole body—just as we found in some of the third-century Syrian examples alongside what appeared to be a separate anointing of the head. It looks, therefore, as though this development may possibly have spread from East to West, or alternatively both regions may have been influenced by similar uses of oil in contemporary pagan traditions.

On the other hand, when we turn to the Syrian sources, we find that the interpretation of the pre-baptismal unction there has changed. Both Chrysostom and Theodore continue to distinguish the anointing of the forehead from the anointing of the whole body that follows it (and according to Chrysostom, a different, perfumed

[6] *De sacramentis* 1.2–3 (*AIR*, p. 100).
[7] *De sacramentis* 1.4 (*AIR*, p. 101).

oil—chrism—is used for the former). Theodore states that the first of these is accompanied by the recitation of the trinitarian formula and constitutes a 'seal' that 'marks you out for ever as the sheep of Christ, the soldier of the King of Heaven': just as a sheep is branded to indicate its owner and a soldier is given a tattoo to indicate the Emperor to whom he owes his allegiance, so too the Christian can be identified as 'a soldier of the true king and a citizen of heaven'.[8] Chrysostom, too, compares this anointing to the branding of a sheep,[9] and also uses the images of both soldier and athlete at this point, but he focuses more on its protective character, which will 'make the devil turn away his eyes'.[10]

Theodore tells us that the same trinitarian formula is used for the anointing of the whole body, but he views this ceremony as symbolic of clothing, 'a sign of the garment of immortality you will receive through baptism'.[11] Chrysostom, on the other hand, describes it in protective terms again, like the previous anointing, intended to 'armour all your limbs and make them invulnerable to any weapons the Enemy may hurl'.[12] Cyril speaks of only one anointing before baptism, that of the whole body, and interprets it both as exorcistic in nature, 'able to pursue all the invisible powers of the wicked one out of our persons', and also as a symbol of the share that the candidate will have in the richness of Christ the true olive tree.[13]

While these explanations of pre-baptismal anointing differ to some extent from one another, what they have in common is that none of them views it in the same way as the earlier Syrian sources had done—as a priestly anointing or as the conferral of the Holy Spirit. Clearly the understanding of the ceremonies of initiation in this region has undergone something of a transformation, and so we now need to look elsewhere in the rite for the themes that were earlier associated with the pre-baptismal anointing.

The profession of faith and immersion

The Eastern and Western traditions retain some of their former characteristics here. The acts of renunciation and adherence to

---

[8] *Baptismal Homily* 2.17-19 (*AIR*, pp. 186-8).

[9] See Paul W. Harkins, *St John Chrysostom: Baptismal Instructions* (Longmans, Green, & Co., London 1963), p. 155.

[10] *Baptismal Homily* 2.22-3 (*AIR*, pp. 166-7).

[11] *Baptismal Homily* 3.8 (*AIR*, p. 194).

[12] *Baptismal Homily* 2.24 (*AIR*, p. 167).

[13] *Mystagogical Catechesis* 2.3 (*AIR*, p. 75).

Christ remain at the beginning of the Eastern rites, while Ambrose attests that in his region the triple immersion in water was still accompanied by a threefold profession of faith in interrogatory form, similar to that evidenced earlier by Tertullian and the *Apostolic Tradition*.[14] (We should note, however, that some Christian groups that rejected trinitarian orthodoxy reverted to just a single immersion at baptism in order to give liturgical expression to their doctrinal position, and some orthodox Christians revised the Eastern act of adherence so that it was made to the Trinity, in order to reflect their position.) On the other hand, in Jerusalem a Western-style interrogatory form of profession of faith has been added at the time of the immersion;[15] and the Syrian baptismal formula ('I baptize you in the name . . .') had already begun to be adopted in Egypt, and would gradually spread westwards during the fifth and sixth centuries.[16] Its introduction there would separate the profession of faith from its original close connection with the immersion and force it into a preliminary position just before it. Because of this change in the rite, it would be easier for later theologians to disregard the vital part that the candidate's own faith had once played in the process of becoming a Christian and to emphasize instead the action of divine grace.

Meanwhile, in Syria itself, Chrysostom reveals that the baptismal formula there had undergone a significant change in wording. Because the active form ('I baptize . . .') had seemed to lay too great an emphasis on the role of the minister, a passive form ('N. is baptized . . .') was now being used instead, and this later became standard in all Eastern rites. Chrysostom also claims that 'by the words of the bishop and by his hand the presence of the Holy Spirit flies down upon you'. The 'words' were the baptismal formula, and the hand was placed on the candidate's head in order to push him or her down under the water. Thus Chrysostom appears to envisage the Holy Spirit being bestowed in the act of immersion itself and not through any ancillary ceremonies, although in line with the new orthodoxy of the period he is also careful to insist that it is 'the indivisible Trinity who bring the whole rite to completion'.[17]

[14] *De sacramentis* 2.20 (*AIR*, pp. 117–18).

[15] *Mystagogical Catechesis* 2.4 (*AIR*, p. 76).

[16] See Paul De Clerck, 'Les origines de la formule baptismale', in Paul De Clerck & Eric Palazzo (eds.), *Rituels: Mélanges offerts au Père Gy* (Editions du Cerf, Paris 1990), pp. 199–213.

[17] *Baptismal Homily* 2.25–6 (*AIR*, pp. 168–9).

Post-baptismal ceremonies

Ambrose refers to an unction of the head with chrism after baptism, during which the bishop simply speaks of God anointing the newly baptized 'into eternal life'. The brevity of his comments on this ceremony suggest that Ambrose himself did not attach much importance to it. He interprets it as a pouring of grace upon the faculties of wisdom in the head, but elsewhere he does allude to the royal and priestly symbolism that Tertullian had earlier emphasized.[18] Ambrose devotes more time instead to defending the appropriateness of the ceremony of the washing of the feet of the newly baptized that immediately follows. He interprets it as providing protection against the liability to sin inherited from Adam.[19] Although none of our other principal sources include it in their rites, there are signs that it was also practised in a number of other places, and it may even at one time have sufficed instead of full immersion in some communities.[20] Finally, Ambrose refers to a 'spiritual sealing' concluding the rite, during which the Holy Spirit was infused at the invocation of the bishop,[21] but he is not explicit as to what this 'sealing' was. It may have been an imposition of hands with prayer (as in Tertullian), a second post-baptismal anointing (as also in *Apostolic Tradition* 21 and later Roman evidence), a simple concluding prayer (as in the later Milanese rites), a sign of the cross, or even a kiss.

Although Chrysostom's rite continued the older Syrian tradition of passing directly from the immersion to the exchange of a kiss and then to the celebration of the eucharist and reception of communion by the newly baptized, Theodore's description includes a reference to a 'sealing' on the forehead at the end of the rite. This apparently involved the use of oil and was accompanied by a trinitarian formula. Theodore understands it as a sign that the Holy Spirit had been bestowed upon the baptized.[22] While some scholars have rejected this passage as a later interpolation into the text, others see it as evidence for the emergence of a post-baptismal unction associated with the gift of the Spirit in the Syrian tradition.

At Jerusalem, something similar to the Western post-baptismal anointing has certainly emerged by this time. However, what Cyril

---

[18] *De sacramentis* 2.24; 3.1; 4.3 (*AIR*, 119-20, 128-9).

[19] *De sacramentis* 3.4-7 (*AIR*, pp. 121-4; see also pp. 27-8).

[20] See Pier Franco Beatrice, *La lavanda dei piedi* (CLV, Rome 1983).

[21] *De sacramentis* 3.8-10 (*AIR*, pp. 124-5).

[22] *Baptismal Homily* 3.27 (*AIR*, pp. 207-9).

describes is not just an anointing of the head, as in Tertullian and Ambrose, but one that also encompassed ears, nose, and chest. Although acknowledging that this anointing (which was done with chrism) was foreshadowed in priestly and kingly anointings in the Old Testament, Cyril likens it to the anointing with the Spirit that Christ received after his baptism. He explains that the anointing of the forehead is done so that the newly baptized may lose the shame of Adam, the ears so that they may hear divine mysteries, the nose so that they may become 'the aroma of Christ to God', and the chest to arm them against the devil.[23] All this suggests that what we have is a conflation of the older Syrian pre-baptismal unction with something similar to the pre-baptismal 'opening' described by Ambrose, but now located instead after the baptism.

All three Eastern bishops—Chrysostom, Cyril, and Theodore— say that the newly baptized do not simply put on their own clothes again but dress in special white garments, as a symbol of the purity of the new life they have begun (Cyril), of Christ whom they have 'put on' internally (Chrysostom), of their future resurrection (Theodore). Ambrose alludes only indirectly to this practice, which reminds him of the shining garments of the transfigured Christ.[24]

Thus, although there are certainly still significant differences in the structure of the rites between East and West (and within each of those regions, too), and different emphases in their interpretation, yet by the close of the fourth century a more homogeneous initiation rite is beginning to emerge, and a rich mixture of images and symbols drawn both from the New Testament and other sources is being used to explain its meaning.

FOR FURTHER READING:

Michel Dujarier, *A History of the Catechumenate: The First Six Centuries* (Sadlier, New York 1979).
Enrico Mazza, *Mystagogy: A Theology of Liturgy in the Patristic Age* (Pueblo Publishing Company, New York 1989).
H. M. Riley, *Christian Initiation. A Comparative Study of the Interpretation of the Baptismal Liturgy in the Mystagogical Writings of Cyril of Jerusalem, John Chrysostom, Theodore of Mopsuestia, and Ambrose of Milan* (Catholic University of America Press, Washington DC 1974).
Edward Yarnold, 'Baptism and the Pagan Mysteries in the Fourth Century', *Heythrop Journal* 13 (1972), pp. 247–67.

[23] *Mystagogical Catechesis* 3 (*AIR*, pp. 79–83).
[24] *AIR*, pp. 28–9, 86–7, 207.

5. From Adult to Infant Baptism

It is not at all certain when baptism began to be extended to infants as well as older children and adults. The first undisputed reference to the custom occurs in North Africa at the beginning of the third century in the writings of Tertullian, who disapproves of it.[1] However, some modern scholars, and notably Joachim Jeremias, have argued that infant baptism was not an innovation at this period but a traditional practice going back to the first century. Much depends upon how references to baptisms of a 'household' in the New Testament (Acts 16.15; 1 Cor. 1.16) should be understood: did that term include very young children or not?

The profession of faith

Whatever the answer to that question, we have seen in earlier chapters that a profession of faith by the candidates themselves was a central element in the baptismal process. When, therefore, infants were to be baptized, this obviously created something of a difficulty. The problem was resolved by allowing someone else to speak on their behalf. Thus *Apostolic Tradition* 21 directs that 'as for those who cannot speak for themselves, their parents or someone from their family shall speak for them.' But neither this nor any other of the earliest sources offers any real theological justification for this practice. For example, the closest that Cyprian came to it was to say that infants' crying constituted their petition to be baptized.[2] Thus it looks as though practice may have preceded doctrine here, perhaps simply as a result of an inchoate desire on the part of Christian parents to have their children share in whatever benefits they believed themselves to enjoy as a result of baptism. Fifth-century sources indicate that a similar action was also taken in the case of adult candidates who had signified their desire for baptism but were too ill to answer for themselves when the time came, and this may even have constituted the precedent for doing this for infants.

It was only later in the writings of Augustine of Hippo (354-430) that a theological justification for infant baptism first appeared that was eventually to become the standard explanation in traditional Catholic theology: belief was not a prerequisite for bap-

[1] *De baptismo* 18 (*DBL*, pp. 8–9).
[2] *Ep.* 64.6.

tism as it was in the case of an adult, but faith was bestowed on the child through the faith of others in the celebration of the rite itself:

> when, on behalf of an infant as yet incapable of exercising faith, the answer is given that he believes, this answer means that he has faith because of the sacrament of faith. . . .
>
> Therefore an infant, although he is not yet a believer in the sense of having that faith which includes the consenting will of those who exercise it, nevertheless becomes a believer through the sacrament of that faith. For as it is answered that he believes, so also he is called a believer, not because he assents to the truth by an act of his own judgment, but because he receives the sacrament of that truth.[3]

As this quotation implies, and as is confirmed from elsewhere in Augustine's writings, a change was made in the wording of the profession of faith when infants were being baptized. Whereas, when the candidate was an adult or older child, this profession was in the form of a series of direct questions and answers ('Do you believe . . .?' 'I believe'[4]), at the baptism of an infant both the questions and the responses made on behalf of the candidate were instead cast in the third person: 'Does he/she believe . . . ?' 'He/she believes.'[5] This variation was enough to cause Augustine's theological opponent Pelagius to argue that, if adults and infants were supposed to be receiving the same baptism, then exactly the same words ought to be used in the rite.[6]

Although there are signs that this form of the profession of faith was also adopted in the case of infants in Spain and France as well as Africa,[7] it did not apparently affect the practice at Rome, which was always particularly conservative in liturgical matters. Consequently, when the Roman rite eventually supplanted all other local rites in the West during the Middle Ages, the use of the adult formula for infants became universal. This effectively reduced the role of the godparent in the rite to that of a mere ventriloquist, supplying a voice for the silent child.

[3] *Ep.* 98.9,10. English translation from Philip Schaff (ed.), *A Select Library of Nicene and Post-Nicene Fathers* 1 (Christian Literature Company, Buffalo 1886), p. 410.

[4] See above, pp. 18–19.

[5] See Augustine, *Ep.* 98.7; *Serm.* 294.12.

[6] See Augustine, *De gratia Christi et de peccato originali* 1.32.35; 2.1.1; 2.21.24.

[7] See J.-Ch. Didier, 'Une adaptation de la liturgie baptismale au baptême des enfants dans l'Église ancienne', *Mélanges de science religieuse* 22 (1965), pp. 79–90.

The trend towards infant baptism as the norm
What is also clear is that even after the practice of infant baptism was adopted, it did not quickly replace adult baptism as the norm everywhere. On the one hand, in North Africa it seems to have become firmly established at an early date. Thus Cyprian in the third century insisted that there was no need to wait until the eighth day after birth to baptize an infant, as some were claiming on the basis of the biblical prescription for circumcision: the mercy and grace of God ought not to be refused to anyone, since all are equal in the gift of grace (*Ep.* 64). On the other hand, we find Gregory Nazianzus in Cappadocia in 381 advising that children should normally be baptized at about the age of three years, when they are able to answer the baptismal questions themselves and can to some extent understand the Christian faith (*Or.* 40.28)! There are also plenty of examples of people from Christian families in the fourth century who were not baptized until they had become adults. Indeed, as we saw in the previous chapter, there was a widespread tendency at that time to delay baptism as long as possible.

By the fifth century, however, the same beliefs that at first had caused people to delay baptism now began to lead them in the opposite direction: if baptism was necessary for salvation, was it not desirable therefore to baptize children as young as possible, lest they should happen to die and forfeit their opportunity for salvation? This tendency was given strong impetus both by the high infant mortality rate in the ancient world and by the theological reflections of Augustine, who argued that because the church practised the baptism of infants, it must follow that babies were thus in need of the remission of sin that baptism brought. Since newborn children had not yet committed actual sins, he concluded that they must have inherited the 'original sin' of Adam: 'What need is there, therefore, for an infant to be conformed to the death of Christ through baptism, if he is not completely poisoned by the serpent's bite?'[8] Augustine was not the first to reason in this way from practice to doctrine. Both Cyprian and Origen in the third century had already drawn similar conclusions from infant baptism,[9] in contrast to earlier Christian theologians who had asserted the purity of newborn children. Augustine not only developed the

---

[8] *De peccatorum meritis et remissione* 1.61.

[9] Cyprian, *Ep.* 64.5; Origen, *Hom. in Lev.* 8; *Hom in Luc.* 14; *Comm. in Rom.* 5.9.

idea more fully, but he added a powerful motivation for conferring baptism at the earliest possible age, since he argued that children dying unbaptized would inevitably be damned, although he believed that they would receive only 'the mildest condemnation'.[10]

It was not long, therefore, before infant baptism became more or less universal throughout the Christian church, and people forgot that baptism had originally been connected with adult conversions. Indeed, some Western texts from the tenth century onwards offer an amusing illustration of the extent to which infant baptisms came to be considered as normative. They direct that infants are to be held in the right arms of their sponsor and adult candidates are to place their foot upon the foot of their sponsor— the latter apparently an attempt to conform as closely as possible to what was done in the case of infants![11] It is also an indication of the extent to which the role of sponsor or godparent had changed: from being the person who presented an adult candidate for baptism and vouched for the genuineness of the conversion that had already taken place in his or her life, the godparent was now the one who held the baby at the ceremony and made the responses to the questions concerning faith on his or her behalf, and in later medieval rites was also charged with the future spiritual upbringing of the child.[12]

The emergence of confirmation

In most cases infants were treated in the same way as adult candidates who were ill or in danger of death: the demands and rituals of the catechumenate were simply eliminated from the process and they proceeded immediately to the baptism itself. It is important to note, however, that in both cases it was the full initiation rite—apart from the catechumenal element—that was usually performed: all the pre- and post-baptismal ceremonies, such as anointing or the imposition of hands, were generally included, and the newly baptized received Holy Communion either at their baptism or soon afterwards, depending upon the urgency of their situa-

---

[10] *De peccatorum meritis et remissione* 1.21.

[11] See J. D. C. Fisher, *Christian Initiation: Baptism in the Medieval West* (SPCK, London 1965), p. 26.

[12] For a detailed study of the role of the godparent, see Joseph H. Lynch, *Godparents and Kinship in Early Medieval Europe* (Princeton University Press, 1986).

tion. The only modifications that might be made were that if the candidates were very ill or weak, rather than being immersed in the water, water could be sprinkled over them instead, and that the whole initiation rite was often performed by a local presbyter rather than waiting until the child could be taken to the bishop (who would normally have presided over it) and so risking the danger of death in the meantime.

The church at Rome, however, was an exception to this rule. Here it was customary for infants to go through the whole catechumenal process, unless they were in imminent danger of death. They would be brought to church at the beginning of Lent and enrolled in the catechumenate; they would be presented on subsequent Sundays during the Lenten season to receive exorcism and to have the Creed, the Lord's Prayer, and the opening verses of the four gospels read to them, even though they were incapable of comprehending what was said; and they would receive the full rite of initiation at Easter.[13]

Obviously, many infants were not healthy enough to wait until Easter each year to be baptized, and so in those cases a similar procedure was adopted as in other places: the initiation rite was performed without delay, and frequently delegated to presbyters. But here, too, Rome constituted an exception to the rule. Rather than the complete rite being performed by a presbyter, as was the case elsewhere, the second post-baptismal anointing (which has no clear parallel in other parts of the world) was reserved exclusively to the bishop, as this extract from a letter written in 416 from Pope Innocent I to Decentius, Bishop of Gubbio, shows:

> Concerning the consignation of infants, it is clear that this should not be done by any but the bishop. For presbyters, although they are priests, have not attained the highest rank of the pontificate. The right of bishops alone to seal and deliver the Spirit the Paraclete is proved not only by the custom of the Church but also by that reading in the Acts of the Apostles which tells how Peter and John were directed to deliver the Holy Spirit to people who were already baptized. For it is permissible for presbyters, either in the absence of a bishop, or when they baptize in his presence, to anoint the baptized with chrism, but only with such as has been consecrated by the bishop: and even then they are not to sign the brow with that oil, for this is reserved to the bishops alone when they deliver the Spirit the Paraclete.[14]

[13] See *DBL*, pp. 154–8, 166–204.
[14] *DBL*, pp. 229–30.

Since churches in other parts of the world did not interpret Acts 8.14–17 to mean that only bishops could bestow the Holy Spirit on the newly baptized, it rather looks as though bishops in Rome were trying to find some justification for retaining the ancient custom of the bishop's personal involvement in every act of Christian initiation, which had been abandoned by other churches in the case of emergency baptisms.

In the Roman situation, such a policy did not really mean the destruction of the unity of the baptismal rite. Presbyters would perform the rest of the rite, including the first communion of the newly baptized, and simply omit the second post-baptismal anointing; and then, provided that the child survived, he or she would be brought to a bishop as soon afterwards as possible in order to receive that missing element. Because dioceses in central Italy were small in area and travel between places relatively easy, the delay between the two parts would usually be very brief. It was only when the practice was extended in later centuries to other parts of the Western Church, as a result of the expansion of Roman influence, that it ceased to work nearly as well. For in northern Europe, dioceses were very large in size and travel often much more difficult, particularly in winter. As a result, the delay between baptism and what was now called 'confirmation' grew much longer, and the two came to be thought of as quite separate sacraments belonging to different points in a person's life.[15]

FOR FURTHER READING:

Kurt Aland, *Did the Early Church Baptize Infants?* (SCM Press, London 1963).
Everett Ferguson, 'Inscriptions and the Origin of Infant Baptism', *Journal of Theological Studies* 30 (1979), pp. 37–46.
Joachim Jeremias, *Infant Baptism in the First Four Centuries* (SCM Press, London 1960).
——— *The Origins of Infant Baptism* (SCM Press, London 1963).
Aidan Kavanagh, *Confirmation: Origins and Reform* (Pueblo Publishing Company, New York 1988).
David F. Wright, 'The Origins of Infant Baptism—Child Believers' Baptism?' *Scottish Journal of Theology* 40 (1987), pp. 1–23.
——— 'How Controversial Was the Development of Infant Baptism in the Early Church?' in James E. Bradley & Richard A. Muller (eds.), *Church, Word, and Spirit: Essays in Honor of Geoffrey W. Bromiley* (Eerdmans, Grand Rapids 1987), pp. 45–63.

[15] For more details of this development, see Fisher, *Christian Initiation: Baptism in the Medieval West*, pp. 120–40.

EUCHARIST

In this section we shall not follow the development of rites and their theology in the same chronological manner as we did in the case of Christian Initiation, where we looked at different regional traditions and traced their gradual coming together. Instead we shall examine several strands of thought and practice that apparently existed alongside one another in nearly every early Christian tradition, and observe how those strands intertwined in the course of the first few centuries.

6. Communion: The Sacred Meal

Traditionally, accounts of the origin of the eucharist in the New Testament have looked to the four descriptions of the Last Supper of Jesus with his disciples on the night before he died (Matt. 27.17–30; Mark 14.12–26; Luke 22.7–38; 1 Cor. 11.23–26). However, for a proper understanding of the roots of Christian eucharistic practice, the Last Supper needs to be set within a broader context, both of the overall tradition of religious meals within Judaism and also of the accounts of other meals that Jesus shared with his disciples during his lifetime and after his resurrection.

There has also been considerable scholarly debate about whether or not the Last Supper was a Passover meal. While the three synoptic gospels state that it was, the Gospel of John places it on the day before the Passover, with Jesus' death occurring on the day of the Passover. However, for our purposes, this question is not particularly crucial. For, even if the Last Supper *were* a Passover meal, no practices that were exclusive to that festive meal seem to have been retained in the primitive Church's eucharistic celebrations, but only those that were common to all formal Jewish meals; and even if it *were not* a Passover meal, it still took place within a Passover atmosphere and context, and so it is not surprising to find images and ideas from that festival turning up in later Christian eucharistic theology.

Religious meals in Judaism
Sharing a meal together has always been one of the main ways in which human beings have expressed friendship and mutual acceptance. Consequently, sacred meals, expressive of the human relationship to the divine, form a part of the ritual practice of many religions. Among the different forms of cultic activities in which the ancient Israelites engaged, for example, were what are called communion-sacrifices. In other forms of Israelite sacrifice the animal or grain offering was handed over completely to God, but in this case part of what was offered was returned to those who had offered it to be eaten by them. In effect, they shared a sacred meal with God as a sign of their acceptance by him through the sacrificial act.

The most important of these communion-sacrifices was the annual Passover celebration. Although in origin the Passover had been a nomadic spring ritual intended to secure fecundity for the flock, it had become for the Israelite people a remembrance of their deliverance by God from slavery in Egypt. Following the prescriptions in Exodus 12, on the day of the festival each family was supposed to take a lamb and offer it for sacrifice in the Temple at Jerusalem, and then consume it together in a ritual meal.

In later Judaism, however, sacred meals were not limited merely to practices connected with the Temple cult. Among the more pious, and especially the Pharisees, every meal came to be thought of as a religious occasion, and included the blessing of God for the gift of the various things to be eaten or drunk. Such people were, moreover, very careful about not only *what* they ate (so as to observe the dietary laws prescribed in the Old Testament) but also *with whom* they shared a meal, since table-fellowship with those regarded as impure would compromise their own ritual purity. It was for this reason that Jesus' behaviour scandalized many of his contemporaries, since, although apparently claiming to be a pious Jew, he ate with the outcasts of society—tax-collectors and sinners (see for example Matt. 9.10–13; Mark 2.15–17; Luke 5.29–32).

Furthermore, it was a regular part of Jewish eschatological imagery to portray the kingdom of God at the end of time in terms of a great banquet, at which all those who enjoyed God's favour would sit down together and feast in abundance. Jesus continued this tradition in his own teaching (see for example Matt. 8.11–12; Luke 13.28–9), and it forms one of the strands in the accounts of the Last Supper: the three synoptic gospels all record in one form or another a saying of Jesus to the effect that 'I shall not drink again of the fruit of the vine until that day when I drink it new in the kingdom of God' (Mark 14.25; see also Matt. 26.29; Luke 22.15,18). Similarly, his feeding miracles and the other meals that he shared must also be viewed in this light, as symbolic anticipations of the future messianic banquet, so that those who eat with him now are assured that they will also feast with him in the age to come.

Thus, all the meals Jesus shared with his followers, and not merely the Last Supper, were seen by the early Christians as expressing not only human fellowship but also the divine acceptance of the participants in the present and the promise of their ultimate place in God's kingdom.

The Ritual Pattern

The accounts of the Last Supper, and also some of the references to meals elsewhere in the New Testament, reveal a pattern that adheres to the common custom followed at all Jewish formal meals. This pattern has been called by some scholars a 'sevenfold shape': at the beginning of the meal, the head of the household, acting on behalf of the gathering, (1) took bread into his hands, (2) said a short blessing, (3) broke the bread, and (4) shared it with all present; and at the end of the meal, he again (5) took a cup of wine into his hands, (6) said a longer form of blessing over it, and (7) shared it with all around the table.

This means, therefore, that the command, 'Do this in remembrance of me' (1 Cor. 11.24, 25), was not intended to initiate some novel ritual practice that the early Christians would not otherwise have done, but was instead a direction that when they performed the customary Jewish meal ritual, they were to do so in future with a new meaning—as a remembrance of Jesus. How 'remembrance' would have been understood in this context we shall pursue in the next chapter. Our primary concern here is to note that ritual meals like this were powerful expressions of the concept of the participants' communion with one another and with God. Their presence at this meal was a sign of their reconciliation to God and their membership among the elect who would one day feast together in God's kingdom, and the intimate fellowship with one another that they experienced around the table was a foretaste, an anticipation, of the union that they would enjoy for ever with God. The whole meal event was thus both a prophetic symbol of the future and also a means of entering into that future in the present.

The vision of the eucharist as fellowship was an important one to St Paul, and he likened the meal to a communion-sacrifice in order to explain the source of the participants' unity with one another: 'The cup of blessing which we bless, is it not a communion in the blood of Christ? The bread which we break, is it not a communion in the body of Christ? Because there is one bread, we who are many are one body, for we all partake of the one bread' (1 Cor. 10.16–17). This explains why he was then so angry about the behaviour of the Christians at Corinth. For at their eucharistic meals, individuals were apparently failing to share the food that they had brought, so that the poor remained hungry while others over-indulged. What was happening was thus the exact opposite of the intimate unity that the meal was supposed to express, so that Paul concludes that 'it is not the Lord's supper that you eat' (1 Cor. 11.20).

Justin Martyr

An account written by Justin Martyr in the middle of the second century provides the earliest complete outline of a eucharistic celebration.

> And on the day called Sunday an assembly is held in one place of all who live in town or country, and the records of the apostles or the writings of the prophets are read for as time allows. Then, when the reader has finished, the president in a discourse admonishes and exhorts (us) to imitate these good things. Then we all stand up together and send up prayers; and as we said before, when we have finished praying, bread and wine and water are brought up, and the president likewise sends up prayers and thanksgivings to the best of his ability, and the people assent, saying the Amen; and the (elements over which) thanks have been given are distributed, and everyone partakes; and they are sent through the deacons to those who are not present. And the wealthy who so desire give what they wish, as each chooses; and what is collected is deposited with the president. He helps orphans and widows, and those who through sickness or any other cause are in need, and those in prison, and strangers sojourning among us; in a word, he takes care of all those who are in need.[1]

Justin's brief reference to the eucharist at the conclusion of the process of Christian initiation adds several further details to this account, the most important of which is that the participants greeted each other with a kiss after the common prayers and before the eucharistic action itself began.[2]

The above description reveals that a number of very significant developments have taken place since New Testament times. First, the meal has entirely disappeared from the celebration, and all that is left are the ritual actions surrounding the bread and wine. It is not clear exactly when this major change took place, and indeed it may have happened at different times in different Christian communities. Some local churches may have retained the eucharistic meal long after others had abandoned it. In some places at least, the meal survived for another century or two in separation from the eucharist itself, as a periodic *agape* or fellowship meal. Nor is it clear why the meal eventually disappeared from the eucharist

[1] *I Apol.* 67.3–7 (*PEER*, pp. 29–30).
[2] See above, p. 14.

everywhere. It may have been as a result of abuses such as those observed by St Paul at Corinth; it may have been because sporadic local bans by the Roman authorities on the meetings of all clubs (which were often centres of political intrigue) prevented Christians from gathering in the evenings; or it may even have been connected with the practical difficulties involved in enabling a large number of people to sit down for a meal together in small houses.

But disappear it did, and as that happened, a profound change was brought about in the Christian experience of eucharistic worship. First, as Justin's account shows, the absence of the meal had a major effect upon the ritual pattern itself. The 'sevenfold shape' found in the New Testament accounts of the Last Supper has been modified in a way that became standard in all later eucharistic rites: the presiding minister now says a prayer of thanksgiving over the bread and wine together, and then shares them with the assembled company. Presumably there seemed no point in retaining distinct actions for the bread and the wine when the two were no longer separated from one another by a meal.

Second, the eucharistic action proper is now preceded by a service of reading, preaching, and intercessory prayer. Scholars have usually understood this to have been a Christian version of the Jewish synagogue liturgy, which included similar elements. They believe that Christians would originally have celebrated this liturgy every Sunday morning, quite separately from the evening eucharistic meal,[3] but when the meal was eventually abandoned, there would have seemed less point in assembling twice, particularly as the ritual surrounding the bread and wine was so brief, and so the two were combined into a single morning service. This theory may well be correct, and we do know from other sources that this later rite was usually celebrated in the morning everywhere. However, we also need to remember that Jewish festive meals could likewise include an informal ministry of the word, with readings, songs, and discourse, and that there are signs in the New Testament of eucharistic celebrations that already had elements of this sort attached to them. There is, for example, the account of the appearance of the risen Jesus to the disciples on the road to Emmaus, where he interprets the scriptures to them before

---

[3] On the choice of Sunday as the Christian day of worship, see below, pp. 75ff.

breaking bread with them (Luke 24.13–35), which is often seen as reflecting the regular pattern of eucharistic worship known to the author. There is the assembly at Troas, where Paul preaches at length and then breaks bread with the company (Acts 20.7–12). And there is also the mention in 1 Cor. 14.26 of 'a hymn, a reading, a revelation, a tongue, or an interpretation' contributed to common worship by the participants, which may refer to the same occasion as the meal described earlier in 1 Cor. 11. So the later practice may be as much an expansion and formalization of this earlier tradition as a fusion of a synagogue-style liturgy with the remnants of the meal ritual.

But even more important than the change in the structure of the rite is the effect that this would have had on what it was that the Christians experienced. There is a world of difference between enjoying fellowship around a table at an evening meal and rising early in the morning in order to engage in a hasty ritual act before setting out for work. Yet even so, something of the close sense of community which had been engendered by the meal fellowship still managed to survive in this new form of the eucharist. We may note, for instance, how Justin stresses the fact that there is a single assembly 'in one place of all who live in town or country', and how the common prayers of the people are concluded with the exchange of a kiss on the lips—an unusually intimate action for those who were unrelated to one another. Justin similarly attaches importance to the assent of the people in the 'Amen' at the end of the eucharistic prayer, and to the inclusion of the absent members in the act of communion. Furthermore, an understanding of the connection between eucharistic communion and the sharing of material possessions with the needy, earlier emphasized by St Paul, is also still apparent in the depositing of monetary gifts with the 'president'.

Unfortunately, however, as we shall see in the later chapters, while the notion of the eucharist as a communion meal continued to find a place in later liturgical texts, the disappearance of the actual meal from eucharistic practice tended to encourage the primary understanding of the rite to shift in a different direction.

44

FOR FURTHER READING:

Joachim Jeremias, *The Eucharistic Words of Jesus* (SCM Press, London 1966).
Jerome Kodell, *The Eucharist in the New Testament* (Glazier, Wilmington 1988).
Xavier Léon-Dufour, *Sharing the Eucharistic Bread: The Witness of the New Testament* (Paulist Press, New York 1987).
Dennis E. Smith & Hal Taussig, *Many Tables: The Eucharist in the New Testament and Liturgy Today* (SCM Press, London 1990).

7. Anamnesis and Epiclesis: The Eucharistic Prayer

Although the precise wording of the Jewish meal prayers over the bread and the cup had probably not yet become firmly fixed during the first century, there was a long established tradition of such prayers of blessing within Judaism, reaching back to Old Testament times. According to this tradition, it would not have been the bread or the wine that was the object of the blessing, but God. In Jewish prayers God was blessed or thanked for what he had done, in rescuing the people from slavery in Egypt, in giving them the promised land and the law to direct their lives, in bringing forth food from the earth and creating the fruit of the vine, and so on. Thus the prayers involved the remembrance (or in Greek, *anamnesis*) of God's mighty works.

In the Jewish world, remembrance was not understood as a purely mental activity. For example, when the penitent thief asked Jesus to 'remember me when you come into your kingdom' (Luke 23.42), he did not expect Jesus merely to think about him, but to act, to do something about his situation. Thus, the worshippers' recalling in prayer of what God had done was not simply nostalgia for the past but led naturally to their petition that God in turn would remember his people, that is, that he would continue to act in the present and the future in similar ways. Because God's nature was constant and unchanging, the one who had liberated Israel from slavery in Egypt would surely also free them from their present sufferings. Hence Jewish prayers of remembrance frequently led into a second half that involved invocation (in Greek, *epiclesis*), calling upon God to continue his saving work among them.

This helps us to comprehend what might have been meant by the saying 'Do this in remembrance of me' (1 Cor. 11.24, 25). Although scholars have often disputed whether it should be understood as 'do this in order that you may remember me' or instead as 'do this in order that God may remember me', the two ideas are really closely connected in Jewish thought and prayer. The disciples' act of remembering Jesus in their eucharistic meals would inevitably have included calling upon God also to remember and to act. We would expect, therefore, that Christianized forms of the Jewish table-prayers would include some recalling of what God had done in Jesus Christ, and some petition for God to bring to completion his saving purposes.

46

The Didache

The New Testament itself does not contain any complete prayer texts of this kind, although there are perhaps hints of them here and there. However, the ancient church order known as the *Didache* has preserved some Christian meal prayers that do what we would expect—recall and request.

About the thanksgiving: give thanks thus:
First, about the cup:
    We give thanks to you, our Father for the holy vine of your child David, which you have made known to us through your child Jesus; glory to you for evermore.
And about the broken bread:
    We give thanks to you, our Father, for the life and knowledge which you have made known to us through your child Jesus; glory to you for evermore.
    As this broken bread was scattered over the mountains and when brought together became one, so let your Church be brought together from the ends of the earth into your kingdom; for yours are the glory and the power through Jesus Christ for evermore.
But let no one eat or drink of your thanksgiving but those who have been baptized in the name of the Lord. For about this also the Lord has said, 'Do not give what is holy to the dogs.'
And after you have had your fill, give thanks thus:
    We give thanks to you, holy Father, for your holy Name which you have enshrined in our hearts, and for the knowledge and faith and immortality which you have made known to us through your child Jesus; glory to you for evermore.
    You, Almighty Master, created all things for the sake of your Name and gave food and drink to mankind for their enjoyment, that they might give you thanks; but to us you have granted spiritual food and drink and eternal life through your child Jesus. Above all we give you thanks because you are mighty; glory to you for evermore. Amen.
    Remember, Lord, your Church, to deliver it from all evil and to perfect it in your love, and bring it together from the four winds, now sanctified, into your kingdom which you have prepared for it; for yours are the power and the glory for evermore. Amen.
    May grace come and this world pass away.
    Hosanna to the God of David.
    If any be holy, let him come; if any be not, let him repent.
    Marana tha. Amen.[1]

Although there is some dispute among scholars as to whether these prayer texts belong to a eucharist or an *agape*, or perhaps both, they have many similarities with what eventually became the standard Jewish table prayers, and so suggest the sort of thing that

[1] *Didache* 9-10 (*PEER*, pp. 23-4).

early Jewish Christians might well have used at their eucharistic meals. We should note in particular the themes of communion and eschatological fulfilment underlying the emphasis in the *epiclesis* parts of the prayers on the Church being gathered together and brought into the kingdom.

The Strasbourg Papyrus

We lack any other prayers that we can with certainty date to the first few centuries. This is probably not because Christians lost or destroyed the texts, but because they never existed in written form. Those responsible for leading eucharistic worship were usually given freedom to improvise their prayers within the limits of the accepted conventions of their local tradition, and it was only in the fourth century that written texts became more common. However, there are a few texts from this later period that may well embody a pattern of prayer used in earlier times, even if they have undergone some later expansion or modification.

One of these, written on papyrus and now preserved at Strasbourg, comes originally from Egypt. Although it only exists in a fragmentary form, it seems to be an early (perhaps even third-century) version of what later became the standard eucharistic prayer of the Coptic church:

to bless (you) . . . (night) and day . . .

(you who made) heaven (and) all that is in (it, the earth and what is on earth,) seas and rivers and (all that is) in (them); (you) who made man (according to your) own image and likeness. You made everything through your wisdom, the light (of?) your true Son, our Lord and Savior Jesus Christ; giving thanks through him to you with him and the Holy Spirit, we offer the reasonable sacrifice and this bloodless service, which all the nations offer you, 'from sunrise to sunset,' from south to north, (for) your 'name is great among all the nations, and in every place incense is offered to your holy name and a pure sacrifice.'

Over this sacrifice and offering we pray and beseech you, remember your holy and only Catholic Church, all your peoples and all your flocks. Provide the peace which is from heaven in all our hearts, and grant us also the peace of this life. The . . . of the land peaceful things towards us, and towards your (holy) name, the prefect of the province, the army, the princes, councils . . .

(About one-third of a page is lacking here, and what survives is in places too fragmentary to be restored.)

(for seedtime and) harvest . . . preserve, for the poor of (your) people, for all of us who call upon (your) name, for all who hope in you. Give rest to the souls of those who have fallen asleep; remember those of whom we make mention today, both those whose names we say (and) whose we do not say

.. (Remember) our orthodox fathers and bishops everywhere; and grant us to have a part and lot with the fair . . . of your holy prophets, apostles, and martyrs. Receive(?) (through) their entreaties (these prayers); grant them through our Lord, through whom be glory to you to the ages of ages.[2]

While this text looks much less like the Jewish forms than the *Didache* prayers were, it still preserves the basic twofold structure of *anamnesis* and *epiclesis*. New features here are the introduction of a reference to sacrifice, and the extension of the petitionary part of the prayer into a full range of intercessions for all sorts of people rather than simply focusing upon the communion of the participants and their admission to the heavenly banquet. These two developments appear to be related to one another, and we shall say more about them in the next chapter.

The Apostolic Tradition

Neither of the texts we have looked at so far concentrates on the saving effects of the death of Christ nor contains an explicit reference to the Last Supper, as we might have expected. Instead, the Strasbourg papyrus seems primarily concerned with the theme of creation, and the *Didache* prayers with the revelation brought by Jesus. However, this was not true of all early eucharistic prayers. The prayer in the *Apostolic Tradition* attributed to Hippolytus centres much more on the theme of redemption, and makes only a passing reference to creation. Although we do not know with any certainty its place and date of origin, this emphasis fits better with Christian thought in the West, which tended to have a less positive view of creation than was the case in the East.

> *Then the deacons shall present the offering to him [the bishop]; and he laying his hands on it with all the presbytery, shall say, giving thanks:*
> The Lord be with you.
> *And all shall say:*
> And with your spirit.
> Up with your hearts.
> We have (them) with the Lord.
> Let us give thanks to the Lord.
> It is fitting and right.
> *And then he shall continue thus:*
> We render thanks to you, O God, through your beloved child Jesus Christ, whom in these last times you sent to us as a savior and redeemer and angel of your will; who is your inseparable Word, through whom you made

[2] *PEER*, pp. 53–4.

all things, and in whom you were well pleased. You sent him from heaven into a virgin's womb; and conceived in the womb, he was made flesh and was manifested as your Son, being born of the Holy Spirit and the Virgin. Fulfilling your will and gaining for you a holy people, he stretched out his hands when he should suffer, that he might release from suffering those who have believed in you.

And when he was betrayed to voluntary suffering that he might destroy death, and break the bonds of the devil, and tread down hell, and shine upon the righteous, and fix a term, and manifest the resurrection, he took bread and gave thanks to you, saying, 'Take, eat; this is my body, which shall be broken for you.' Likewise also the cup, saying, 'This is my blood, which is shed for you; when you do this, you make my remembrance.'

Remembering, therefore, his death and resurrection, we offer to you the bread and the cup, giving you thanks because you have held us worthy to stand before you and minister to you.

And we ask that you would send your Holy Spirit upon the offering of your holy Church; that, gathering her into one, you would grant to all who receive the holy things (to receive) for the fullness of the Holy Spirit for the strengthening of faith in truth; that we may praise and glorify you through your child Jesus Christ, through whom be glory and honor to you, to the Father and the Son, with the Holy Spirit, in your holy Church, both now and to the ages of ages.[3]

All our other evidence indicates that the account of the Last Supper (or narrative of institution, as it is called by liturgical scholars) gradually began to appear in eucharistic prayers from about the middle of the fourth century onwards. Hence, it seems likely that at least that part of the above text, together with the section immediately after it, 'Remembering . . . cup', was added to the prayer around that period, especially as it seems to interrupt the series of thanksgivings for redemption and the calling of the people of God. Some scholars have argued that the petition for the sending of the Holy Spirit is also a later addition, because its language is more consistent with fourth-century thought (as also is the trinitarian ascription at the end). Once again, we will consider further both these matters in a subsequent chapter.

What is thus left as the older nucleus of the prayer has the familiar twofold structure of *anamnesis* and *epiclesis*. While the first part has a stronger Christological emphasis than we saw in the other prayers, the second part retains the primitive focus on petition for the fruits of communion.

[3] *AT* 4 (*PEER*, pp. 34–5).

50

Later developments

The late fourth century saw not only the gradual emergence in all eucharistic prayers of secondary elements of the sort that we can see in the prayer from the *Apostolic Tradition* and of extensive intercession similar to that in the Strasbourg papyrus, but also the widespread introduction of an expression of praise of the creator culminating in the angelic hymn, 'Holy, holy, holy, Lord God of hosts . . . ', an adaptation of Isaiah 6.3 found in the Jewish synagogue liturgy. There are signs to suggest that this unit may have formed a part of some Egyptian eucharistic prayers from a much earlier date and spread from there to other regions of the world in the general process of assimilation and liturgical standardization that is characteristic of orthodox Christianity after the Council of Nicea in 325. Because all these elements were not always inserted in exactly the same place in the various local prayer patterns, the process resulted in quite different structures of eucharistic prayer in the different regions of East and West, and these variations persisted in later centuries.

FOR FURTHER READING:

Allan Bouley, *From Freedom to Formula: The Evolution of the Eucharistic Prayer from Oral Improvisation to Written Texts* (Catholic University of America Press, Washington DC 1981).
Geoffrey Wainwright, *Eucharist and Eschatology* (Epworth Press, London 1971).

8. 'The bloodless sacrifice'

The notion of sacrifice as the normal means of human interaction with the divine was fundamental to all religions in the ancient world, and early Christianity was no exception to that rule. However, in the Christian tradition the material offering of animals was replaced by a more 'spiritualized' or 'bloodless' concept of sacrifice, which influenced early eucharistic worship in several different ways.

'Pure' sacrifice: the offering of life and of praise

The roots of this idea can already be seen within first-century Judaism. The writings of Philo of Alexandria, who was strongly influenced by Stoic and Platonic philosophy, reveal a vision of the only sacrifice worthy of God as being that of a pure mind and soul offering itself to God; and the sectarian Jewish community at Qumran similarly regarded the offering of a life of virtue and of words of divine praise, 'the fruit of the lips' (Hosea 14.2) as an acceptable temporary substitute for the Temple cult, from which they had separated themselves on the grounds that it had become corrupt.

Thus, in the New Testament we find, for example, St Paul exhorting his readers 'to present your bodies as a living sacrifice, holy and acceptable to God, which is your spiritual worship' (Romans 12.1). Similarly, the author of the Epistle to the Hebrews, while on the one hand insisting that Christ's own oblation of himself has put an end to the need for propitiatory sacrifice once and for all (Heb. 10.10–18), can still call for Christians to offer to God both praise (citing Hosea) and a life of love for others: 'Through him [i.e, Jesus] then let us continually offer up a sacrifice of praise to God, that is, the fruit of lips that acknowledge his name. Do not neglect to do good and to share what you have, for such sacrifices are pleasing to God' (Heb. 13.15–16).

It is not surprising, therefore, that in Christian writings of the second and third centuries all prayer, and not just the eucharist alone, was understood as constituting a sacrifice of praise offered to God.[1] Nevertheless, it was inevitable that among all the acts of worship offered to God by Christians the eucharist should come to be viewed as the preeminent sacrifice of praise. Indeed, it was a standard part of their polemic against the Jews that Christians were

[1] See below, pp. 71–2.

the ones who truly fulfilled what they understood to be a prophecy in Malachi 1.11 ('from the rising of the sun to its setting my name is great among the nations, and in every place incense is offered to my name, and a pure offering') because they offered the eucharist to praise and glorify God in every place, while the Jews had only offered their sacrifices in the Temple in Jerusalem.[2] An early example of this way of thinking occurs in the *Didache*, which instructs Christians to come together on Sunday, 'break bread, and give thanks, having first confessed your transgressions, that your sacrifice may be pure'. Those who have quarrelled must also be reconciled to one another before joining in the celebration 'that your sacrifice may not be defiled'.[3] Here the 'pure offering' is seen as requiring purity of life as well as words of praise and thanksgiving, a message that had been articulated by the Old Testament prophets and reiterated in the teaching of Jesus (see, for example, Mark 7.1–23).

It is this idea of the eucharist as the sacrifice of praise that we find articulated in the eucharistic prayer of the Strasbourg papyrus with its explicit quotation from Malachi, which we looked at in the previous chapter,[4] and it recurs in more subtly expressed forms in other liturgical texts.

Gift-sacrifice: the offering of bread and wine

The transition in the primary understanding of the eucharist from 'sacred meal' to 'holy food', which we shall examine more fully in the next chapter, also had an effect upon Christians' understanding of the sort of sacrifice they thought was offered in the eucharist. While the idea that it was the act of praise that they were offering to God persisted in both liturgical texts and theological writings in later times, there emerged alongside it the notion that the bread and wine constituted the Christian offering. We can see this concept already in Justin Martyr. While affirming that 'prayers and thanksgivings made by worthy men are the only sacrifices that are perfect and well-pleasing to God', at the same time Justin linked these with the offering of the 'bread of the thanksgiving and likewise the cup of the thanksgiving' as constituting the fulfilment of the material oblations of the Old Testament.[5] The fact that the

---

[2] See for example Justin Martyr, *Dialogue with Trypho* 41 (*PEER*, p. 27).

[3] *Didache* 14 (*PEER*, p. 24).

[4] See above, p. 47.

[5] *Dialogue with Trypho* 41.3; 117.2 (*PEER*, pp. 27–8).

worshippers themselves brought the bread and wine with them from their homes to be used in the eucharist (just as they had earlier contributed the food and drink for the full eucharistic meal) would obviously have further encouraged the idea that these elements formed the substance of the sacrifice.

This concept was given a unique twist by Irenaeus of Lyons in the late second century, who saw the eucharistic oblation of bread and wine as symbolic of the offering of the firstfruits of creation, which had been mandated in the Old Testament: 'The Lord gave directions to his disciples to offer first-fruits to God from God's own creatures, not as though God stood in need of them, but that they themselves may be neither unfruitful nor ungrateful.'[6] It is clear that here the prime purpose of the offering is seen to be the spiritual benefit that the act brings to those who perform it.

The notion that the bread and wine were the material of the Christian oblation also found its way into liturgical texts. In the *Apostolic Tradition*, for example, they are described as 'the offering', and the eucharistic prayer explicitly states: 'we offer you the bread and the cup. . . .',[7] an expression that would often be copied in later liturgical texts.

Memorial-sacrifice: the remembrance of Christ's self-offering

So far we have been considering themes that led to the understanding of the eucharist as being a sacrifice in its own right, as it were. Christians of course recognized that they had been constituted into a priesthood (1 Peter 2.5,9; Rev. 1.6; 5.10; 20.6) and made worthy to offer sacrifice to God only through Jesus Christ, but the ways of thinking outlined above did not make any *direct* connection between the sacrificial nature of the eucharistic rite or its elements and the sacrificial character of Christ's death.

Nevertheless, from the first the eucharist was understood as a memorial of Christ's sacrifice. This is a fundamental strand in the New Testament tradition. Both Paul and the synoptic gospels associate the origin of the eucharist with the Last Supper, which they understand as a Passover meal with its inevitable sacrificial overtones, and although they differ as to the exact words of Jesus

---

[6] *Adversus haereses* 4.17.5; see also 4.18.1. English translation from David N. Power, *Irenaeus of Lyons on Baptism and Eucharist* (Grove Books, Nottingham 1991), p. 15.

[7] See above, pp. 48–9.

over the bread and cup, they all record them as pointing to a sacrificial interpretation of the act: 'this is my body/my body which is for you . . .' 'blood of the covenant, which is poured out for many/new covenant in my blood. . . .' Indeed, Paul goes on to identify the Christian rite explicitly as a memorial of Christ's passion: 'For as often as you eat this bread and drink the cup, you proclaim the Lord's death until he comes' (1 Cor. 11.26).

In the second century Justin Martyr made a connection between the oblation of the bread and the memorial of Christ's passion: 'The offering of fine flour . . . which was handed down to be offered by those who were cleansed from leprosy, was a type of the bread of the thanksgiving, which our Lord Jesus Christ handed down to us to do for the remembrance of the suffering which he suffered for those who are cleansed in their souls from all wickedness of men, so that we might give thanks to God. . . .'[8] In the same way, the phrase about the offering of the bread and cup in the eucharistic prayer of the *Apostolic Tradition* quoted earlier in this chapter follows directly upon the narrative of the Last Supper and is linked with remembrance, here extended to include the resurrection as well: 'Remembering, therefore, his death and resurrection, we offer to you the bread and the cup. . . .'

Once again, other eucharistic prayers would follow this lead. In all these instances, therefore, the idea of the remembrance of Christ's sacrificial death is being combined with the pre-existing notion of the eucharist itself as a sacrifice to create what we might perhaps describe as the concept of the rite as a memorial-sacrifice.

The writings of Cyprian, the third-century bishop of Carthage, may possibly mark a further significant change in this idea:

> For if Jesus Christ, our Lord and God, is himself the chief priest of God the Father, and has first offered himself a sacrifice to the Father, and has commanded this to be done in commemoration of himself, certainly that priest truly discharges the office of Christ, who imitates that which Christ did; and he then offers a true and full sacrifice in the Church to God the father, when he proceeds to offer it according to what he sees Christ himself to have offered.[9]

[8] *Dialogue with Trypho* 41.1; see also 117.3 (*PEER*, pp. 27–8).

[9] *Ep.* 63.14; English translation from Alexander Roberts & James Donaldson (eds), *The Ante-Nicene Fathers* 5 (Charles Scribner's Sons, New York 1919), p. 362.

55

Some scholars would interpret Cyprian as saying that in the eucharist the priest (by which he means the bishop) offers the same sacrifice that Christ offered on the cross, i.e., that the bishop 'offers Christ'. While this is certainly the first place where the bishop is said to 'discharge the office of Christ', other scholars do not think that the image should be taken quite so literally, that it means no more than something like: 'just as Christ offered himself as a sacrifice, so too does the bishop offer the Church's sacrifice in memory of him'.

Whatever Cyprian may have meant, however, some later Christian writers unquestionably use language that does identify the Church's sacrificial act very closely indeed with the sacrifice of Christ. Thus, for example, Cyril of Jerusalem states, 'we offer Christ who has been slain for our sins';[10] and Gregory Nazianzus says that 'you sacrifice the Master's body and blood with bloodless knife'.[11] John Chrysostom, however, in one of his homilies struggled between this way of talking and the conviction that there was only one sacrifice of Christ, even though there were many celebrations of the eucharist:

> Do we not offer every day? We offer indeed, but making a remembrance of his death, and this [remembrance] is one and not many. How is it one and not many? In as much as that [sacrifice] was once for all offered, [and] carried into the holy of holies. This is a figure of that [sacrifice] and this remembrance of that. For we always offer the same, not one sheep now and tomorrow another, but always the same thing, so that the sacrifice is one. And yet by this reasoning, since the offering is made in many places, are there many Christs? But Christ is one everywhere, being complete here and complete there also, one body. As then while offered in many places, he is one body and not many bodies, so also [he is] one sacrifice. He is our high priest, who offered the sacrifice that cleanses us. That we offer now also, which was then offered, which cannot be exhausted. This is done is remembrance of what was then done. For (saith he) 'do this in remembrance of me.' It is not another sacrifice, as the high priest, but we offer always the same, or rather we perform a remembrance of a sacrifice.[12]

Ancient liturgical texts themselves, on the other hand, were much more conservative in their language, and spoke rather in

[10] *Mystagogical Catechesis* 5.10 (*AIR*, p. 92).
[11] *Ep.* 171.
[12] *Hom. in Heb.* 17.6; English translation from Philip Schaff (ed.), *A Select Library of the Nicene and Post-Nicene Fathers of the Christian Church* 14 (Charles Scribner's Sons, New York 1906), p. 449.

terms of celebrating the memorial of Christ's sacrifice. While a very close relationship was seen between Christ's sacrifice and the Church's offering, some distinction between the two was also maintained.

Propitiatory sacrifice

We saw earlier that a petitionary element seems to have been integral to the basic structure of the earliest eucharistic prayers, and that it appears to have focused on praying for the gathering together of the communicants into one body in readiness for the coming of God's kingdom. Once the theme of sacrifice had made its way into eucharistic prayers, it would have been natural for some connection to be made between the act of offering and these petitions. Christians would have been reminded of other kinds of Old Testament sacrifices in which offerings were made in the hope of propitiating God's justifiable anger against sinful human conduct and averting divine punishment, or with the intention of securing other benefits from God. Hence, it is not surprising to find that the scope of these petitions begins to be enlarged.

The ancient East Syrian prayer of Addai and Mari, for example, prays for 'remission of debts, forgiveness of sins' as well as for 'the great hope of resurrection from the dead, and new life in the kingdom of heaven, with all who have been pleasing in your sight'.[13] The Strasbourg papyrus, as we saw in the previous chapter, included a very wide range of objects of intercession which it explicitly connected with the Church's offering: 'Over this sacrifice and offering we pray and beseech you, remember your holy and only Catholic Church, all your peoples and all your flocks. . . .'[14]

Similarly, in describing the pattern of eucharistic prayer with which he was familiar, Cyril of Jerusalem in the fourth century said:

> Then, when the spiritual sacrifice—this worship without blood—has been completed, we beg God over the sacrifice of propitiation for general peace among the churches, for the right order of the world, for the kings, for soldiers and allies, for the sick and the afflicted, and in short we all make entreaty and offer this sacrifice for all who need help. Next we recall those who have gone to rest before us, and first of all the patriarchs, prophets,

[13] *PEER*, p. 43.
[14] See above, p. 47.

apostles and martyrs, so that God may listen to our appeal through their prayers and representations. After that, we pray on behalf of the holy fathers and bishops and in general for all amongst us already gone to their rest, for we believe that these souls will obtain the greatest help if we make our prayers for them while the holy and most awesome sacrifice is being offered.[15]

This idea led both to greatly expanded intercession in eucharistic prayers everywhere and also, in Western Christianity, to the emergence of special celebrations of the eucharist on weekdays with the intention of securing some particular benefit. One of the earliest forms of this was a celebration on the anniversary of a person's death so as to intercede for the repose of their soul.

FOR FURTHER READING

Robert J. Daly, *The Origins of the Christian Doctrine of Sacrifice* (Fortress Press, Philadelphia 1978).

R. P. C. Hanson, *Eucharistic Offering in the Early Church* (Grove Books, Nottingham 1979).

Kenneth W. Stevenson, *Eucharist and Offering* (Pueblo Publishing Company, New York 1986).

Frances M. Young, *The Use of Sacrificial Ideas in Greek Christian Writers from the New Testament to John Chrysostom* (Philadelphia Patristic Foundation, Cambridge, Mass., 1979).

[15] *Mystagogical Catechesis* 5.8–9 (*AIR*, pp. 91–2).

9. Holy Food

There is another strand of thought present in the New Testament which would be strongly developed in later centuries, and that focuses not on the meal as event, but on the bread and wine themselves as spiritual food. We can perhaps even see this emerging in the difference between the remembered words of Jesus over the cup of wine in Paul and in Mark. Paul recalls the words as being 'this cup is the new covenant in my blood' (1 Cor. 11.25), suggesting a vision of the eucharist as effective action, the shared meal sealing a covenant between God and those partaking of it which had been made by the shedding of the blood of Jesus, just as in the Old Testament covenants were sealed in sacrificial blood. Mark's version, on the other hand, speaks more directly of the wine as 'This is my blood of the covenant' (14.24), which seems to imply that the presence of the Lord was attached more to the food than to the meal event.[1] This way of thinking is even more clearly revealed in the 'I am the bread of life' discourse of John 6.

Alongside their continued understanding of the eucharist as a communal action, therefore, the writings of the second and third centuries also develop this way of thinking. Thus, for example, one of the prayers in the *Didache* speaks of the gift of 'spiritual food and drink';[2] and Justin Martyr says:

> we call this food 'thanksgiving' . . . . For we do not receive these things as common bread or common drink; but just as our Savior Jesus Christ, being incarnate through the word of God, took flesh and blood for our salvation, so too we have been taught that the food over which thanks have been given by a word of prayer which is from him, (the food) from which our flesh and blood are fed by transformation, is both the flesh and blood of that incarnate Jesus.[3]

Moreover, although we have suggested in an earlier chapter[4] that the primary reason for the practice described by Justin of carrying some of the bread and wine to those unable to be present was to draw them into the celebration, yet the abstraction of the elements from the eucharistic action as a whole would inevitably encourage people to think of them as somehow special in them-

---

[1] See Willi Marxsen, *The Beginnings of Christology* (Fortress Press, Philadelphia 1979), p. 110.

[2] See above, p. 46.

[3] *1 Apol.* 66.1–2 (*PEER*, p. 29).

[4] See p. 43.

selves. This understanding can clearly be seen in the custom
known to us from various sources from the third century onwards
of people taking home a little of the bread from the eucharist (and
perhaps the wine also, though difficulties in storing that safely
made it less common) to consume at home on weekdays.

It is of course possible to think of this practice, too, like the
communion of the absent, as being simply an extension of the
Sunday celebration. Indeed, Basil of Caesarea in the fourth century
says that the person receiving communion in this way 'must
believe that he duly takes and receives it from the hand that first
gave it'.[5] Nevertheless, the language used by the early Christians
unquestionably reveals that special significance was seen in the elements themselves. Like Justin, for example, Irenaeus in the late
second century says that 'the bread . . . when it receives the
invocation of God is no longer common bread, but the eucharist,
consisting of two realities, the earthly and the heavenly. . . .'[6]

Sometimes Christians expressed the nature of the eucharistic
elements by the use of words such as 'figure', 'sign', 'symbol', or
'type'. Cyril of Jerusalem, for instance, states that Christ's 'body
has been bestowed on you in the form (typos) of bread, and his
blood in the form (typos) of wine', and that communicants 'taste
not bread and wine but the sign (antitypon) of Christ's body and
blood'.[7] Similarly, Ambrose of Milan testifies that the eucharistic
prayer of his church spoke of the elements as being 'the figure
(figura) of the body and blood of our Lord Jesus Christ'.[8] On the
other hand, they sometimes used strongly 'realistic' language,
affirming that the bread and wine were truly the body and blood of
Christ, as we saw above in the quotation from Justin. We should
not make too much of these differences in language, however. In
the ancient world a sign or symbol was not thought of as being
something quite different from the reality which it represented, but
on the contrary was understood as participating in some way in
that reality itself. Moreover, the same writers who use 'symbolic'
language also usually have no hesitation in using more 'realistic'
language on occasion. Thus Cyril can state quite unequivocally:
'Do not, then regard the bread and wine as nothing but bread and

[5] Ep. 93.
[6] Adversus haereses 4.18.5 (Power, Irenaeus of Lyons on Baptism and
Eucharist, p. 15).
[7] Mystagogical Catechesis 4.3; 5.20 (AIR, pp. 85, 93).
[8] De sacramentis 4.21 (AIR, p. 136).

wine, for they are the body and blood of Christ as the master himself has proclaimed.'[9]

Strangely enough, the use of 'realistic' language among Christians appears to be older than the more careful 'symbolic' language, and to have arisen in order to counteract heretical claims that Christ was not truly human and did not really suffer and die on the cross. Ignatius of Antioch in the early second century, for example, says that some 'abstain from eucharist and prayer because they do not acknowledge the eucharist to be the flesh of our Saviour Jesus Christ which suffered for our sins and which the Father raised by his goodness'.[10] Thus eucharistic realism arose out of Christological realism, and no contradiction was seen between saying that the bread and wine were the body and blood of Christ 'spiritually', 'symbolically', or 'really'. This whole development of eucharistic thought would also have been encouraged, of course, by the removal of the full meal from the eucharistic celebration, which would have caused more emphasis to fall on the bread and wine when they were no longer part of a larger whole.

Consecration

The identification of the bread and wine as in some sense the body and blood of Christ inevitably raised the theological question as to how these ordinary things became this holy food. Justin Martyr's answer to this question, as we have seen earlier in this chapter, appears to say that it was the result of thanks having been given over the food 'by a word of prayer which is from him'. However, the original Greek here is ambiguous, and so it would be equally possible to translate the phrase as 'by a prayer of the word that is from him' or as 'by the prayer of the Word [*Logos*, i. e., Christ] who is from him', and what Justin means to say has been variously explained by scholars. Does the 'him' refer to God or to Christ? Is it saying that the actual form of words used comes from Christ or God, or that the prayer includes an invocation of the *Logos* on the bread and wine, or just that the prayer has its origin in God's word? The last seems the most likely, especially as there is a similar statement in 1 Tim. 4.4–5, that 'nothing is to be rejected if it is received with thanksgiving; for then it is consecrated by the word of God and prayer'.

[9] *Mystagogical Catechesis* 4.6 (*AIR*, p. 85).
[10] *To the Smyrnaeans* 7.1.

It was inevitable that the idea that the bread and wine were the body and blood of Christ would in time affect the language of the second half of eucharistic prayers, the part that we earlier termed the *epiclesis*. As we have seen, at first this petitionary element tended to focus on the communicants themselves. Eventually, however, petitions began to appear which requested God to act in relation to the bread and wine as well as, or in some cases instead of, the congregation. Sometimes God was asked to send the second person of the Trinity—the *Logos*—and sometimes it was the Holy Spirit who was called down. This was because Christians at first did not distinguish as sharply between the two as they did after the fourth-century trinitarian debates. They often thought of the Holy Spirit as being the spirit of the risen Christ, and so tended to use the two terms somewhat interchangeably.

Thus, in the eucharistic prayer attributed to Sarapion, the mid-fourth-century bishop of Thmuis in Egypt, God is asked: 'let your holy Word come on this bread, O God of truth, that the bread may become body of the Word; and on this cup, that the cup may become blood of the Truth; and make all who partake. . . .'[11] On the other hand, the petition in the eucharistic prayer of the *Apostolic Tradition* asks God to 'send your Holy Spirit upon the offering of your holy Church. . . .'[12] While some scholars judge this to be a fourth-century addition to the text, others believe that 'the offering' here refers to the action, the eucharistic sacrifice of praise, rather than more narrowly to the elements alone. Whatever the truth of that particular case, it was only after the fourth-century debates that orthodox churches of the East began to attach great importance to the inclusion of an explicit *epiclesis* of the Holy Spirit on the eucharistic elements.

We can also see a gradual development in what the Spirit is expected to do in connection with the bread and wine. At first, imprecise verbs like 'bless' and 'sanctify' are found, as in the ancient East Syrian eucharistic prayer of Addai and Mari: 'may your Holy Spirit, Lord, come and rest on this offering of your servants, and bless and sanctify it. . . .'[13] The fourth-century prayer of St Basil, however, adds the Greek verb *anadeiknumi* ('show forth'): 'And we, sinners and unworthy and wretched, pray you,

[11] *PEER*, pp. 77-8.
[12] See above, p. 49.
[13] *PEER*, p. 43.

our God, in adoration that in the good pleasure of your goodness your Holy Spirit may descend upon us and upon these gifts that have been set before you, and may sanctify them and show them forth as holy of holies'.[14] Similarly, Theodore of Mopsuestia explains that the bishop entreats God 'that the Holy Spirit may come and that grace may descend from on high on to the bread and wine that have been offered, so showing us that the memorial of immortality is truly the body and blood of our Lord.'[15] This reflects a shift towards what might be called an 'epiphany' understanding of consecration, in which the Spirit is invoked on the community and on the gifts in order that the presence of Christ may be revealed in them.

On the other hand, a number of other fourth-century sources use language about eucharistic consecration that suggests instead the idea of a change or conversion in the elements of bread and wine rather than a revealing of what was hidden. Cyril of Jerusalem, for example, implies that the eucharistic prayer known to him asked God to send the holy Spirit to 'make' the elements the body and blood of Christ,[16] and we have already seen the verb 'become' used in this way in the eucharistic prayer of Sarapion. Even stronger language is found in the eucharistic prayer which is attributed to John Chrysostom, although first known to us from a eighth-century manuscript:

> we pray and beseech and entreat you, send down your Holy Spirit on us and on these gifts set forth; and make this bread the precious body of your Christ, changing it by your Holy Spirit, Amen; and that which is in this cup the precious blood of your Christ, changing it by your holy Spirit, Amen; . . . .[17]

In the writings of Ambrose in the West in the fourth century we find similar language about a change in the eucharistic elements. In contrast to the Eastern sources, however, Ambrose understands this to be effected not by an invocation of the Holy Spirit (which seems to have been absent from eucharistic prayers in the West) but by the recitation of the words of Christ in the narrative of

---

[14] PEER, p. 71; but the translation 'make them holy of holies' has been amended here in order to make its true meaning clearer.

[15] Baptismal Homily 5.12 (AIR, p. 246).

[16] Mystagogical Catechesis 5.7 (AIR, p. 91).

[17] PEER, p. 133.

institution, which was already a part of the eucharistic prayer in Milan where he was bishop:

> How can something which is bread be the body of Christ? Well, by what words is the consecration effected, and who words are they? The words of the Lord Jesus. All that is said before are the words of the priest: praise is offered to God, the prayer is offered up, petitions are made for the people, for kings, for all others. But when the moment comes for bringing the most holy sacrament into being, the priest does not use his own words any longer: he uses the words of Christ. Therefore, it is Christ's word that brings this sacrament into being.[18]

The belief that eucharistic consecration was effected by the recitation of the narrative of institution subsequently became universal in Western Christian doctrine, and distinguished it from Eastern Christian theology, which continued to attach consecratory significance to the *epiclesis* of the Holy Spirit.

FOR FURTHER READING:
William R. Crockett, *Eucharist: Symbol of Transformation* (Pueblo Publishing Company, New York 1989), ch. 2.
Nathan Mitchell, *Cult and Controversy: The Worship of the Eucharist Outside Mass* (Pueblo Publishing Company, New York 1982), ch. 1.

[18] *AIR*, p. 133.

10. 'Let all mortal flesh keep silence'

The second half of the fourth century witnessed a further change in eucharistic practice that was nearly as profound as the change brought about by the disappearance of the meal at the end of the New Testament period. This was the emergence of an attitude of great awe and fear directed towards the eucharistic elements, together with a decline in the frequency of the reception of communion.

The introduction of the numinous

When looking at the development of Christian initiation, we saw that a major change took place in the way in which the rituals were performed after the Peace of Constantine in the fourth century. The lack of a genuine conversion experience, or even of a full understanding of the significance of becoming a Christian, led to a strong dramatizing of the baptismal ceremonies in order to produce a profound emotional effect upon the candidates. Something similar also occurred in connection with the eucharist. The members of the Church were no longer an elite group of highly committed believers, but a much larger mass of nominal converts, many of whom lacked a deep understanding of the Christian faith and an awareness of the conduct that was appropriate at its liturgical assemblies. According to John Chrysostom, for example, they pushed and pulled one another in an unruly manner during the services; they gossiped with one another; young people engaged in various kinds of mischief; and pickpockets preyed upon the crowd.

In order to impress upon worshippers the solemnity of what was happening in the eucharistic rite and of the reverent behaviour appropriate for such an occasion, therefore, the style of eucharistic celebrations underwent a significant alteration. They became much more formal and elaborate; they used such things as ceremonial actions, vesture, processions, and music in order to make an impression upon the congregation; and in word and action they stressed the majesty and transcendence of God and the divinity of Christ present in the eucharistic mystery. This last development was probably also influenced in part by the need to combat the Arian heresy, which relegated Christ to a subordinate position, and its beginnings can be seen in the opening address of the eucharistic prayer of St Basil:

It is fitting and right, fitting and right, truly it is fitting and right, I AM, truly Lord God, existing before the ages, reigning until the ages; you dwell on high and regard what is low; you made heaven and earth and the sea and all that is in them. Father of our Lord and God and Savior Jesus Christ, through whom you made all things visible and invisible, you sit on the throne of your glory; you are adored by every holy power. . . .[1]

As we saw in the previous chapter, the prayer also goes on to describe the worshippers as 'sinners and unworthy and wretched'.[2]

Later prayers would develop this sort of language much further still, but at this stage it was in preaching and teaching about the eucharist rather than in the liturgical texts themselves that the twin notes of the majesty of God and awe at Christ's presence in the sacrament were most strongly struck. This can be seen in Cyril of Jerusalem, in Theodore of Mopsuestia, and most strongly in John Chrysostom, who repeatedly speaks of the 'dreadful sacrifice', of the 'fearful moment' when the mysteries as accomplished, and of the 'terrible and awful table' that should only be approached with fear and trembling. Cyril of Jerusalem also gives practical advice to the newly baptized on the reverent manner in which to receive communion:

So when you come forward, do not come with arm extended or fingers parted. Make you left hand a throne for your right, since your right hand is about to welcome a king. Cup your palm and receive in it Christ's body, saying in response *Amen*. Then carefully bless your eyes with a touch of the holy body, and consume it, being careful to drop not a particle of it. For to lose any of it is clearly like losing part of your own body. . . . After partaking of Christ's body, go to the chalice of his blood. Do not stretch out your hands for it. Bow your head and say *Amen* to show your homage and reverence, and sanctify yourself by partaking also of Christ's blood. While your lips are still moist with his blood, touch it with your hands and bless your eyes, forehead, and other organs of sense.[3]

We can see here that not only are the eucharistic elements to be treated with great reverence when they are consumed but that they are also regarded as objects of power which can be used to confer blessing on a person's body and protect it against evil and sickness.

In short, the attitudes instilled in eucharistic worshippers at this time are well summed up in the Cherubic Hymn from the ancient

[1] *PEER*, p. 70.
[2] See above, p. 62.
[3] *Mystagogical Catechesis* 5.21–2 (*AIR*, pp. 94–5).

Liturgy of St James, an English paraphrase of which by Gerard Moultrie is found in a number of modern hymnbooks:

> Let all mortal flesh keep silence,
> and with fear and trembling stand;
> ponder nothing earthly minded,
> for with blessing in his hand
> Christ our God to earth descendeth,
> our full homage to demand. . . .

Non-communicating attendance

Fourth-century preachers were concerned not only about the conduct of Christians during the eucharistic rite itself but also about their whole way of life. They were disturbed that many worshippers seemed unaware of the high standards of ethical behaviour demanded by Christianity, and so they stressed the essential connection between liturgy and life, warning the congregation against coming to communion while leading unworthy lives. John Chrysostom was particularly vigilant in this regard, frequently emphasizing the sincerity and purity of soul necessary to approach the supper of the Lord: 'With this, approach at all times; without it, never!'[4] He advised those who were guilty of sin to leave the service before the eucharistic action itself began. The aim of preaching such as this was not to *dis*courage the reception of communion, but rather to *en*courage higher standards of Christian living.

Unfortunately, as so often happens, the results were exactly the opposite of the intentions of the preachers. Many people preferred to give up the reception of communion rather than amend their lives. Thus began the practice of non-communicating attendance at the eucharist. Contrary to Chrysostom's advice, they apparently stayed until the time for communion and then left the church. The ecclesiastical authorities were eventually forced to accept this practice, and they began to make provision in the rites at the time of the communion for a formal dismissal of non-communicants in order to encourage a more orderly departure.

This development had a significant effect upon people's understanding of the eucharist, since it severed the act of communion from the rest of the eucharistic action. It made it possible for people to think of the eucharist as complete and effective

[4] *Hom. in Eph.* 3.4.

without the need for them to participate in the reception of the bread and wine, and thus prepared the way for the idea that liturgy was something that the clergy did on their behalf, which ultimately did not even require their presence. We can see the beginnings of this notion in John Chrysostom. His very assertion that there are some times when there is no difference at all between the roles of priest and people is a tacit admission that there are other times when there most definitely is a difference:

> But there are occasions when there is no difference at all between the priest and those under him; for instance, when we are to partake of the awful mysteries. . . . And in the prayers also, one may observe the people contributing much. . . . Again, in the most awful mysteries themselves, the priest prays for the people and the people also pray for the priest; for the words 'with thy spirit' are nothing else than this. The offering of thanksgiving again is common: for neither doth he give thanks alone, but also for all the people. . . .[5]

Eucharist as drama

For those who now began to receive communion only infrequently in a year and for the rest of the time attended without communicating, the eucharist not only ceased to be a communal action, but was not even viewed as food to be eaten. Instead, it became principally an object of devotion, to be gazed on from afar. It is not surprising, therefore, that ancient liturgical commentators began to interpret the rite in terms of a drama that unfolded before the eyes of the spectators.

We can see this happening in the preaching of Theodore of Mopsuestia. He envisages the whole eucharistic liturgy, from the presentation of the bread and wine to the reception of communion, as a ritual allegory reenacting the events of Jesus's passion, death, burial, and resurrection. This leads him to reinterpret various liturgical actions as representing elements and moments in that story. So, for example, the bringing up of the bread and wine is no longer seen as symbolizing their offering by the people but as Christ being led to his passion; and the deacons spreading cloths on the altar 'remind us of winding-sheets'.[6] For Theodore, the climax of the rite is at the *epiclesis* of the Holy Spirit during the

---

[5] *Hom. in 2 Cor.* 18.3; English translation from Philip Schaff (ed.), *A Select Library of the Nicene and Post-Nicene Fathers of the Christian Church* 12 (Christian Literature Company, New York 1889), pp. 365–6.

[6] *Baptismal Homily* 4.25 (*AIR*, pp. 227–8).

eucharistic prayer, since 'this is moment appointed for Christ our Lord to rise from the dead and pour out his grace upon us all'. The bread and wine which have until now symbolized the dead body of Jesus become his risen body.[7] Finally, the breaking of the bread that follows the prayer symbolizes Christ's sharing of himself in his various resurrection appearances so that everyone was able to come to him, just as the communicants are now able to do.[8]

FOR FURTHER READING:

Edmund Bishop, 'Fear and Awe attaching to the Eucharistic Service' in R. H. Connolly, *The Liturgical Homilies of Narsai* (Cambridge 1909), pp. 92-7.
J. G. Davies, 'The Introduction of the Numinous into the Liturgy: An Historical Note', *Studia Liturgica* 8 (1971/72), pp. 216-23.
Nathan Mitchell, *Cult and Controversy*, ch. 2.

[7] *Baptismal Homily* 5.11-12 (*AIR*, pp. 245-6).
[8] *Baptismal Homily* 5.17-18 (*AIR*, p. 249).

LITURGICAL TIME

In this final section we will look at the ways that the early Christians used the various cyclical patterns of time with which they were familiar—the day, the week, and the year—in order to give expression to different aspects of their beliefs.

11. Daily Prayer

Times for prayer

The New Testament implies that at least some early Christians engaged in a regular pattern of daily prayer, since it speaks of the disciples as 'persevering with one accord in the prayer' (Acts 1.14) and 'persevering in . . . the prayers' (Acts 2.42). Similar phrases occur in Acts 6.4, Rom. 12.12, and Col. 4.2. None of these references, however, reveal what this pattern might have been. While there are allusions to specific times of prayer, including the sixth hour (Acts 10.9), night (Acts 12.5,12), and midnight (Acts 16.25), it is impossible to know whether these were established hours for Christian prayer, or instead were merely occasioned by the particular circumstances being described in the story.

We might expect the first Christians to have continued to observe whatever were the customary Jewish times of daily prayer, but there seems to have been a variety of practice among Jews of the first century: some appear to have prayed twice a day, morning and evening, but others three times a day, either morning, noon, and evening, or morning, afternoon (3 p.m.), and evening. Thus, examining Jewish prayer patterns does not help us very much in discovering what the oldest Christian customs were.

The first clear evidence that we have for Christian times of prayer comes from the *Didache* (8.3), which instructs its readers to pray three times a day, although it does not say exactly when those three times were to be: presumably it expected them to know that already. Morning, noon, and evening were probably what were intended, as these are mentioned in some third-century sources, although other Christians appear to have preferred to adjust these times slightly to correspond to the principal divisions of the day in the Roman Empire: the third, sixth, and ninth hours (9 a.m., 12 noon, and 3 p.m.). All these sources add prayer at night to the cycle, and evidence from North Africa reveals the emergence of a conflation of the two methods of threefold daily prayer into a fivefold pattern that would become more or less universally prescribed in the fourth century: morning, third hour, sixth hour (noon), ninth hour, and evening.

Eschatological expectation

We might assume that the Christian adoption of this custom of daily prayer at specific hours was simply the result of the power of tradition: the first converts had prayed at set times when they were

Jews, continued to do so when they became Christians, and passed the tradition on to succeeding generations. While this may certainly be part of the reason for the practice, much more meaning was associated with it than that.

The earliest Christians confidently expected the return of Christ and the consummation of the kingdom of God within the immediate future, and believed that they were called to be alert and watchful at all times for that final salvific event. Just as servants were expected to stay awake and watch for the return of their master, so they too were to be vigilant for the return of their Lord (see Mark 13.32–37; Luke 12.35–40). Several New Testament texts suggest that prayer was regarded as the proper mode of this eschatological vigilance. 'Watch and pray that you may not enter into temptation', says Jesus in the Garden of Gethsemane (Mark 14.38 & parallels); and the same advice in repeated in the epistles: 'persevere in the prayer, being watchful in it with thanksgiving' (Col. 4.2); 'praying at all times in the Spirit, and to that end being watchful in all perseverance . . . ' (Eph. 6.18). The discipline of prayer at regular, fixed times, therefore, was an expression of their constant readiness for the end time, as it also appears to have been among certain Jewish groups of the period.

The offering of life

As time went by, however, and this event failed to happen, the eschatological aspect of daily prayer naturally began to grow dim. Although traces of it can still be seen in Christian writings of the late second and early third centuries, the main justification for maintaining the traditional times of daily prayer has now shifted. Authors of this period continue to repeat St Paul's precept to 'pray without ceasing' (1 Thess. 5.17) as the only absolute rule binding upon Christians, but they tend to see its fulfilment as being in the turning of the whole of one's life into an act of worship offered to God, and the observance of the fixed hours of prayer as a part of this broader obligation.

There are precedents for this way of thinking in the New Testament itself. For example, St Paul urges Christians to 'present your bodies as a living sacrifice, holy and acceptable to God . . . ' (Rom. 12.1). Moreover, the idea that Christians constituted a priesthood (1 Peter 2.5,9; Revelation 1.6; 5.10; 20.6) also encouraged them to view the oblation of their life as their priestly sacrifice to God. Christians of the second and third centuries therefore naturally thought of their times of prayer as part of this offering. Thus Tertullian spoke of prayer as 'a spiritual oblation which has abolished the former sacrifices', and Origen saw the daily sacrifices of the Old Testament (described there as 'perpetual') as finding their true fulfilment in the perpetual prayer of Christians.[1]

The 'cathedral' office: the sacrifice of praise

After the Peace of Constantine in the fourth century Christians began to celebrate publicly certain of the daily hours of prayer which they had previously observed either individually or with their families. The hours generally chosen were the morning and the evening, partly because these were the only ones for which it was practical for most people to gather together (the other times occurred during the working day, and it was not easy or always safe to venture out for prayer at night), and partly because these were now seen as the Christian equivalent of the daily morning and evening sacrifices prescribed by God in the Old Testament. Modern scholars have labelled these public services as the 'cathedral' office, because they were understood by those taking part in them as being the Church's sacrifice of praise and priestly intercession for the needs of all. They were therefore composed of two principal elements: hymns and psalms of praise, and prayers for the Church and the world. The hymns were usually unchanging from day to day. Pss. 148–150 seem to have formed the nucleus of the morning praise everywhere, while in the evening the hymn *Phos hilaron*, 'Hail gladdening light', was often used as the lamps were lit and thanksgiving offered for the natural light of the day, for the lamplight in the darkness of the night, and for the illumination brought by the light of Christ.

The idea that these two occasions constituted the fulfilment of the Old Testament sacrificial law led in the fifth century to the introduction of a regular offering of incense in the services, in accordance with Exod. 30.7–8: 'And Aaron shall burn fragrant incense on it [the altar]; every morning when he dresses the lamps he shall burn it, and when Aaron sets up the lamps in the evening he shall burn it, a perpetual incense before the Lord throughout your generations.'

[1] Tertullian, *De oratione* 28; Origen, *Hom. in Num.* 23.3; *Contra Celsum* 8.17, 21–2.

73

Prayer in the desert: ceaseless meditation

At least from the end of the second century, if not sooner, there were some who regarded the observance of fixed hours of prayer as no more than a second-best way of fulfilling the apostolic injunction to pray without ceasing. The ideal was truly uninterrupted praying. This attitude seems to have been particularly prevalent in Alexandria among those Christians who had come under the influence of the philosophy of Plato and the Stoics, and it was extensively developed by Clement of Alexandria. Although he admitted the necessity of set times of prayer for those not very far advanced in the spiritual life, yet for those who would be perfect Christians (or 'Gnostics' as he calls them), prayer was to be a state of continual communion with God:

> During his whole life the Gnostic in every place, even if he be alone by him-self, and wherever he has any of those who have exercised the like faith, honours God, that is, acknowledges his gratitude for the knowledge of the way to live. . . . Holding festival, then, in our whole life, and persuaded that God is altogether on every side present, we cultivate our fields, praising; we sail the sea, hymning. . . .
>
> Now if some assign fixed hours for prayer—as, for example, the third, and sixth, and ninth—yet the Gnostic prays throughout his whole life, endeavouring by prayer to have fellowship with God. And briefly, having reached to this, he leaves behind him all that is of no service, as having now received the perfection of one who acts by love.[2]

This approach to prayer was appropriated by the ascetics who went out into the deserts of Egypt and Syria in the fourth century, and whose aim was to maintain there as near as possible a cease-less vigil of prayer, punctuated only by the minimal interruption for food and sleep. Not only did they thus devote more time to actual praying than other Christians, but their concept of prayer was also radically different. They did not see themselves as engaged in offering the Church's sacrifice of praise or praying for the needs of the world, but instead as individuals seeking their own salvation through constant meditation and petition for spiritual growth. Thus the form of the praying was also quite different from that of the 'cathedral' office. Whether praying alone or with others, they used the Old Testament psalms as the basis for their

[2] Clement of Alexandria, *Stromata* 7.7; English translation from William Wilson, *The Writings of Clement of Alexandria* 2 (T & T Clark, Edinburgh 1872), pp. 431, 432, 435.

meditation, because they understood the Book of Psalms to be a prophecy of Christ, and they alternated the reading of a psalm (or its recitation from memory) with a period of silent prayer. In this manner they gradually worked their way through the whole 150 psalms in order.

Monastic prayer: the traditions fused

The fourth century also saw the gradual emergence of religious communities who did not make their home in desert regions but remained in towns and cities in close contact with the Church around them. The foundations of their prayer life were the older Christian traditions of praying at least five times each day and again during the night. Inevitably, however, they were influenced both by the spirituality of the desert and also by the practice of the 'cathedral' office around them. As a result, their forms of daily prayer became hybrid in character. They included the selective psalmody of the 'cathedral' services as well as the consecutive recitation of psalms of the desert tradition, and the monks and nuns thought of themselves both as singing hymns to God and as meditating on the psalms at the same time.

This particular spirituality did not remain restricted to such communities alone. Because nearly every important Christian bishop of the second half of the fourth century had lived as a monk at one time or another during his career, the form of spiritual life that they advocated to ordinary lay people was essentially monastic in character. In addition to attendance at the 'cathedral' office every day, therefore, people were encouraged to maintain the other traditional times of prayer individually, and to learn the psalms and recite them frequently. In this way, the fusion of early Christian, 'cathedral', and desert traditions passed into the mainstream of Christian spirituality of the succeeding ages.

FOR FURTHER READING:
Paul F. Bradshaw, *Daily Prayer in the Early Church* (SPCK, London & Oxford University Press, New York 1981).
Robert F. Taft, *The Liturgy of the Hours in East and West* (Liturgical Press, Collegeville 1986).

12. Sunday

New Testament evidence

The New Testament contains only three possible allusions to the early Christian observance of Sunday, and it is not completely clear how each of these should be interpreted. Acts 20.7–12 describes a gathering 'to break bread' that took place 'on the first day of the week' and continued past midnight. But was this the regular occasion for Christian worship every week, or did it take place on that day only because St Paul was about to depart? In 1 Cor. 16.2, the apostle exhorts his readers to put aside a monetary offering 'on the first day of every week'. But was this day chosen for the activity because the Christians were regularly gathering together for worship then, or for some quite different reason? Rev. 1.10 states that the author was 'in the Spirit on the Lord's day'. But does the expression 'Lord's day' refer to Sunday, as it certainly seems to do when it occurs again in *Didache* 14, or has it some quite different meaning here?

However, in spite of the absence of any completely indisputable evidence for the Christian observance of Sunday prior to the middle of the second century, most scholars believe that it was adopted as early as the first generation of believers.

The Christian Sabbath?

Some have thought that Christians replaced Saturday with Sunday as their Sabbath day in order that they might differentiate themselves from other Jews. Others have disagreed, and have argued that, while Jewish-Christians may perhaps have gone on observing an actual weekly Sabbath, Gentile Christians who adhered to St Paul's view of the Jewish Law as no longer binding upon them would have had no interest in keeping any day of the week as a Sabbath. Moreover, while early Christian writings certainly retained the Jewish image of the Sabbath rest, they viewed it as coming at the end of time and did not apply it to a day of the week. These scholars conclude that Sunday was therefore not the Christian Sabbath but the occasion chosen for their regular gatherings for corporate worship, and so did not involve a cessation from work on that day, which in any case would have been impossible for most of them, since it was a regular working day (it was only in the fourth century that the Emperor Constantine made Sunday a public holiday).

Commemoration of the resurrection

So then, why did the Christians choose that particular day of the week? Some have thought that it was because, according to the gospel accounts, Jesus had risen from the dead on 'the first day of the week', and hence Sunday was intended primarily as a commemoration of the resurrection. This certainly seems to be a part of the answer, and it continued to have this function in later centuries. At Jerusalem in the fourth century, for example, there was a special early service every Sunday morning at the site of Christ's tomb when one of the gospel accounts of the resurrection was read. This practice subsequently spread to other parts of the world. But other evidence suggests that there was more to the significance of this day than just the remembrance of Christ's resurrection, however important that may have been.

The day of the eucharist

One of the most remarkable aspects of early Christian worship was the restriction of the celebration of the eucharist to Sunday alone. Apart from a single reference in Acts 2.46 to the first Christians meeting day by day to break bread together in their homes (which may well be a bit of idealizing by the author), all other evidence from the first three centuries points to the conclusion that the only days on which Christians celebrated the eucharist were Sundays, together with saints' days as those emerged in local churches. Even in the fourth century, many churches resisted the extension of the celebration of the eucharist to other days. While some churches turned the regular Wednesday and Friday services of the word (see below, pp. 78–9) into full celebrations of the eucharist, others did not, and still others adopted a compromise, in which communion was given at those services, but with bread and wine consecrated at the Sunday eucharist. While Western Christians did gradually move towards celebrating the eucharist on any day of the week, Eastern Christians have continued to adhere to the older tradition of a full celebration only on Sundays and other holy days.

Early Christian writings do not explain the reason for this restriction of the eucharist to Sundays, but it must have been ancient and firmly rooted for it to survive for so long. One is reminded of the appearance of the risen Christ on the road to Emmaus (Luke 24.13–35), which not only took place on a Sunday but included a meal in which 'he was known to them in the breaking of the bread'. This story suggests that early Christians experienced the presence of Christ in their Sunday eucharistic celebration, but we do not of course know which element came first. Was it because the empty tomb had been discovered on a Sunday that early Christians decided to meet regularly for a eucharistic meal on that day, and then encountered Christ in the celebration? Or was Sunday already the regular day for their weekly meal together—a custom perhaps even initiated by Jesus in his lifetime—and because they experienced the presence of their risen Lord then, they believed that the resurrection had taken place on the first day of the week? We will almost certainly never know the answer, but what does seem to emerge is that Sunday was not just the occasion for a commemoration of a past event—the resurrection—but the celebration of a present experience—communion with the risen Christ.

The eighth day

Sunday had a reference to the future as well as to the past and to the present in the early Church. Not only did the eucharist itself have an eschatological dimension, symbolizing the messianic banquet at the end of time, but the titles Christians gave to the day also expressed that same vision. It was known by some not just as 'the first day of the week' but as 'the eighth day'. Since in Jewish thought the number seven symbolized perfection, the concept of an eighth day obviously signified something greater still. Because according to Ps. 90.4 a thousand years was like a single day in the sight of the Lord, they imagined that this world would last for six days (i.e., six thousand years), to be followed by a seventh day, a thousand years when Jesus would reign as Messiah, and then an eighth day, a final golden age that would last for ever. Hence, in giving the same title to Sunday, they were envisaging it as a symbolic foretaste of that eschatological time to which they looked forward in hope.

This concept also explains another early title for the day, 'the Lord's day'. Old Testament prophets had used a similar expression, 'the day of the Lord', to refer to the end of time, and the Christian term seems to imply the notion that Sunday was a symbolic anticipation of the age to come when Christ would be Lord of all, just as he was already Lord in the Church. For the same reason, both kneeling for prayer and fasting were forbidden on this day in the early Church, as they were thought incompatible with its joyful character as a foretaste of the kingdom of God. Conversely,

Sunday was considered the day most appropriate for almsgiving. We noted at the beginning of this chapter St Paul's injunction to set aside money for the needy on the first day of the week, and Justin Martyr's account of a eucharistic celebration revealed the continuation of this practice in the second century.[1] While it was certainly desirable to be charitable every day of the week, it was particularly suitable on Sunday, the day which proclaimed the welcome that the poor and needy would receive in God's kingdom.

The day of the epiphany of the Church

Finally, we need to note the emphasis that early Christians laid on *all* members of a local church assembling together on Sundays. As we have noted in earlier chapters, Justin Martyr stressed that there was a single assembly 'in one place of all who live in town or country', and that the bread and wine were taken to those who were unable to be there so that they might be drawn into that assembly. And for some centuries afterwards it remained unthinkable for there normally to be more than one eucharist in a church each Sunday—a tradition maintained to this day by Eastern Christians—or more than one eucharist in a town. Even when it did later become necessary in large cities to have several congregations, attempts were made to retain links between them. In Rome, for instance, when the Pope presided at a eucharistic celebration, he would send a little piece of the consecrated bread (called the *fermentum*) to the other celebrations of the eucharist in the city, so that their essential unity could be symbolized.

All this suggests that Sunday was seen as the day for the manifestation, or epiphany, of the Church. During the rest of the week the Church was dispersed and hidden, as its individual members went about their life and work in different places. But on Sunday the Church came together and revealed itself in the celebration of the eucharist, with each member occupying his or her place in the assembly, or affirming their membership through communion in the bread and wine brought to them. In this way, they were also laying claim to their place at the Lord's table in the future kingdom of God.

Wednesday and Friday

Didache 8.1 directed Christians not to fast on Mondays and Thursdays (the regular Jewish fast-days) but on Wednesdays and

---

[1] See above, pp. 41–3.

Fridays, and this custom continued to be widely observed in later centuries, with regular services of the word also taking place at the ninth hour (about 3 p.m.) on these days. It has traditionally been assumed that Christians made this change in order to differentiate their practices more clearly from those of the Jews and merely picked these days at random. However, this assumption did not take into account how deeply rooted liturgical customs tend to be, and how unlikely random change would be. More recent scholars have concluded, therefore, the first Christian converts may have been influenced in their choice by the solar calendar in use among the Essene Jewish community at Qumran, in which Wednesday and Friday had a certain prominence, even though these days were not marked by fasting or by any special liturgical assemblies at Qumran so far as we are aware. The substitution of the ninth hour instead of the morning for a service of the word, as on the Jewish fast-days, appears to have been made in order to commemorate the death of Jesus at that hour (Matt. 27.46–50; Mark 15.34–7; Luke 23.44–6).

FOR FURTHER READING:

D. A. Carson (ed.), *From Sabbath to Lord's Day* (Zondervan, Grand Rapids 1982).
Willy Rordorf, *Sunday* (SCM Press, London 1962).
H. Boone Porter, *The Day of Light: The Biblical and Liturgical Meaning of Sunday* (SCM Press, London 1960 = Pastoral Press, Washington DC 1987).

13. Easter and Pentecost

Early Christian sources reveal two quite distinct modes of celebrating Easter. The one which ultimately became universal was to keep the feast on the Sunday after the Jewish Passover and to focus its celebration upon the resurrection of Jesus Christ from the dead, which—according to the four canonical gospels—had taken place on the first day of the week. The other ancient form of the celebration is attested chiefly in second-century sources deriving from Asia Minor. This tradition makes Easter a memorial of the death of Jesus, and situates the feast instead at the time of the Jewish Passover itself, during the night from 14 to 15 Nisan. Because of their attachment to the fourteenth day of the Jewish month, those who followed this custom were called 'Quartodecimans' by other Christians.

The traditional scholarly consensus tended to be that the Sunday celebration was the older of the two (perhaps even going as far back as the apostolic age itself, even though it is only explicitly attested from the second century onwards) and was the one observed by the mainstream of the Christian tradition. The Quartodeciman custom was judged to be no more than a second-century local aberration from this norm, brought about by an apparently common tendency among some early Christians to 'Judaize', a practice already criticized by St Paul in the first century (see, for example, the Letter to the Galatians).

On the other hand, some scholars have claimed that the Quartodeciman practice began at a much earlier date as a Jewish-Christian adaptation of the Passover festival, while others have gone further still and argued that the celebration of Easter on a Sunday was a considerably later development than is often supposed—that it was not adopted at Rome until about 165, although it may have emerged in Alexandria and Jerusalem somewhat earlier. Prior to this time, these churches would have known no annual Easter observance at all. If this theory is correct, then it effectively reverses the conclusions reached by the majority of earlier scholars, so that Quartodecimanism is not some local aberration from a supposed normative practice dating from apostolic times, but is instead the oldest form of the Easter celebration.

It is not difficult to understand how leaders of communities of early Christians that did not at first observe an annual commemoration of the death and resurrection of Christ might have desired to adopt the practice that they saw among the Quartodecimans. Nor is it hard to appreciate why they would have preferred to locate this innovation on the Sunday immediately following the Passover rather than on the actual feast itself: since Sunday was already the occasion of their regular weekly celebration of the paschal mystery, it would obviously be easier to develop that existing liturgical day than to persuade congregations to embrace a completely new event.

The meaning of the feast

The above hypothesis certainly helps to explain several otherwise somewhat puzzling features of the early Christian observance of Easter, and not least the meaning that was given to it. For not only in Quartodeciman circles but also at first among those who kept the feast on Sunday, the original focus of the celebration was not on the resurrection of Christ but rather on 'Christ, the Passover lamb, sacrificed for us'. While this seems a perfectly natural direction for a feast situated on the Jewish Passover to have taken, it appears to be a less obvious path for the Sunday celebration, if it were not originally derived from the Quartodeciman custom.

The image of Christ as the Passover lamb is found in 1 Cor. 5.7, and also underlies John's Gospel. There Jesus is identified as 'the Lamb of God' near the beginning (1.36) and is said to have died on the cross on the day of the preparation of the Passover (i.e., 14 Nisan) at the hour when the lambs for the feast were being slaughtered (19.14ff.). In addition, the soldiers are said to have refrained from breaking the legs of the dead Jesus in order that the scripture requiring no bone of the Passover lamb to be broken (19.32-6; cf. Exod. 12.46; Num. 9.12) might be fulfilled.

That this theme was central to the Quartodecimans' celebration can be seen not merely from the date on which Easter took place, but also from the emphasis on the suffering and death of Christ found in their writings. Indeed, they even claimed that the name of the feast, Pascha (which in reality is simply a transliteration of the Aramaic form of the Hebrew *pesach*), was derived from the Greek verb *paschein*, 'to suffer'. Precisely the same interpretation and theology of the feast occur in the writings of those early Christians who kept Easter on Sunday.

At the end of the second century in Alexandria, however, we encounter a different understanding of the feast, one that focused upon 'passage' rather than 'passion'—the passage from death to life. Clement of Alexandria describes the Passover as humanity's passage 'from all trouble and all objects of sense';[1] and Origen in the middle of the third century explains this interpretation more fully: 'Most, if not all, of the brethren think that the Pascha is named Pascha from the passion of the Savior. However, the feast in question is not called precisely Pascha by the Hebrews, but *phas[h]*. . . . Translated it means "passage." Since it is on this feast that the people goes forth from Egypt, it is logical to call it *phas[h]*, that is, "passage."'[2]

Fourth-century Alexandrian Christians tended to combine the two interpretations. Although this change of focus may in part be simply the result of a more accurate exegesis of the Hebrew scriptures, it is also in line with the general tendency among Alexandrian theologians to allegorize and de-historicize the Christian mysteries. We may also add the influence that would have been exercised by the day on which the feast occurred: Sundays throughout the year were primarily associated with the resurrection of Christ to new life rather than with his death. Moreover, evidence from both Egypt and Syria in the third century reveals the beginnings of a trend to view the Easter observance as a *triduum*, a three-day celebration of the transition from death to resurrection. But in order to understand this development, we must first take a look at the origins of the paschal fast.

The paschal fast and the triduum

The limited evidence that exists for the form of the Quartodeciman observance suggests that the period of fasting which in Jewish tradition preceded the eating of the Passover meal at nightfall on 14 Nisan was extended by the Christians into a vigil during the night, so that their celebration of the feast with a eucharistic meal only began at cockcrow (i.e., around 3 a.m.) after the Jewish festivities were over. The reason for the choice of this particular hour is not explained in the Quartodeciman sources, but it seems likely that it has its roots in watching and waiting for the predicted return of Christ to complete his work of redemption, just as Jewish tradition expected the coming of the Messiah to be at Passover time.

---

[1] *Stromata* 2.11.51.2; English translation from Raniero Cantalamessa, *Easter in the Early Church* (Liturgical Press, Collegeville 1993), p. 52.

[2] *On the Pascha* 1; English translation from Cantalamessa, *Easter in the Early Church*, p. 53.

The Sunday celebration also included a preceding day of fasting and a night vigil culminating in the celebration of the eucharist. Once again, these two elements are easier to comprehend when understood as appropriations from the Quartodeciman practice. For there does not seem to be anything intrinsic to the nature of the Sunday celebration to have given rise either to a day of fasting or to a vigil. Moreover, primitive Christian tradition regarded all Saturdays, like Sundays, as inappropriate for fasting—no doubt a vestige of respect for the Sabbath that had been inherited from Judaism—and thus the introduction of a fast on a Saturday would have constituted a significant break with tradition which could not have been done lightly.

It was not long, however, before the Saturday fast became extended in some Christian communities. As we have seen, it was already a well established tradition for Christians to keep every Wednesday and Friday throughout the year as days of fasting, and so some churches began to join the regular Friday fast and the Saturday paschal fast together to create a continuous two-day preparatory fast before the Easter festival. Christians in Egypt and Syria went even further and created a six-day fast from Monday until the end of the Saturday vigil. The third-century Syrian church order known as the *Didascalia Apostolorum* gives a detailed explanation of the practice. This document maintains that Judas was paid for his betrayal 'on the tenth day of the month, on the Monday' (5.17.8), and so it was as though Jesus had already been seized on that day, in fulfilment of the Pentateuchal requirement to take a lamb on the tenth day of the month and keep it until the fourteenth (Exod.12.3, 6). It then continues:

> Therefore you shall fast during the days of the Pascha from the tenth, which is a Monday; and you shall sustain yourselves with bread and salt and water only, at the ninth hour, until the Thursday. But on the Friday and on the Saturday fast completely, and do not taste anything. You shall come together and watch and keep vigil all the night with prayers and intercessions, and with reading of the Prophets, and with the Gospels and with Psalms, and fear and trembling, and with earnest supplication, until the third hour in the night after the Saturday; and then break your fasts. . . .[3]

This passage is interesting in several respects. First, we may note that because the term Pascha is understood to refer to the pas-

[3] 5.18-19.1 (Brock & Vasey, *The Liturgical Portions of the Didascalia*, p. 28).

sion of Christ, it is used to denote the period of the memorial of Christ's suffering and death, and not the celebration of his resurrection, as is also the case in other early sources: strictly speaking, the Pascha ends at the conclusion of the fast and vigil. Second, the biblical prescriptions about the timing of the Passover have been adapted to fit a quite different chronology, which may possibly be an indication that this section of the text has Quartodeciman roots. Third, this chronology would clearly make Friday the day on which Christ died (even though it does not seem as yet to be marked by any special liturgical observance), and therefore begin to point the Easter vigil in the direction of being a memorial more of the resurrection than of the death of Christ or of the whole paschal mystery. This transition of meaning is in fact made clear by a another reference to the end of the vigil later in the text: 'after which eat and enjoy yourselves, and rejoice and be glad, because Christ, the pledge of our own resurrection, is risen. . . .'[4] Finally, although the church order does prescribe six days of fasting, a distinction is still maintained between the older two-day fast and the other days of the week, and this is also emphasized in other parts of the document: 'Especially incumbent on you therefore is the fast of the Friday and Saturday. . . . Fast then on the Friday, because on that day the People killed themselves in crucifying our Saviour; and on the Saturday as well, because it is the sleep of the Lord; for it is a day which ought especially to be kept with fasting. . . .'[5]

A similar development can also be seen in the Egyptian sources. In the passage from Clement of Alexandria cited above as the earliest evidence for the understanding of the feast as 'passage', he too spoke of it as having begun 'on the tenth day'; and Origen clearly viewed the paschal events as extending over three days, in fulfilment of Hosea 6.2, even if they were not yet liturgically celebrated in this way: 'Now listen to what the prophet says: "God will revive us after two days, and on the third day we shall rise and live in his sight." For us the first day is the passion of the Savior; the second on which he descended into hell; and the third, the day of resurrection.'[6]

In the light of all this, it is not surprising to find in sources from the late fourth century the emergence of the liturgical obser-

---

[4] 5.19.7 (ibid., p. 28).

[5] 5.19.6,9-10 (ibid., p. 28).

[6] *Hom. in Exod.* 5.2; English translation from Cantalamessa, *Easter in the Early Church*, p. 55.

vance of Good Friday as the memorial of Christ's death, with Easter itself now being regarded as essentially the celebration of his resurrection. To this was often added Holy Saturday as the commemoration of his burial and/or descent into Hell. This development seems to have begun at Jerusalem itself in connection with the sacred sites associated with the passion and resurrection, and spread slowly from there to other parts of the Church.

Pentecost

A number of sources at the end of the second century indicate the existence of a fifty-day season following Easter. Called Pentecost, it was regarded as a time of rejoicing, and every day was treated in the same way as Sunday, that is, with no kneeling for prayer or fasting. Since the Jewish feast of Pentecost was celebrated only on the fiftieth day after the Passover, and did not involve any special treatment of the intervening period, this season appears to be a purely Christian innovation, intended to extend the celebration of Easter. At first no particular emphasis appears to have been placed on the fiftieth day itself by Christians, but in the fourth century we find that day being celebrated as a commemoration of the gift of the Holy Spirit, in accordance with Acts 2. In some places the celebration of the day also included the Ascension of Christ, but towards the end of the century a separate feast of the Ascension on the fortieth day (Acts 1.3) emerged in a number of places and became almost universal early in the fifth century. Thus the original unity of the fifty-day season was gradually broken down, and regular fasting resumed after the fortieth day, or in some places even before it.

FOR FURTHER READING:

Raniero Cantalamessa, *Easter in the Early Church* (Liturgical Press, Collegeville 1993).
Thomas J. Talley, *The Origins of the Liturgical Year* (Pueblo, New York 1986), Part 1.

14. Christmas, Epiphany, and Lent

There is no firm evidence for the Christian observance of either 25 December or 6 January before the fourth century. Of course, it is always possible that one or both of these festivals was in existence at an earlier date, but if so, we have no knowledge of it. What is clear from the fourth-century evidence, however, is that at first no local church kept both these occasions: Rome and North Africa celebrated 25 December, while all other churches seem to have observed 6 January. It is only towards the end of the century that we find churches beginning to add the other date to their calendar.

25 December

The earliest evidence for the existence of a feast of the Nativity of Jesus on this date is its inclusion in what is known as the Roman Chronograph of 354, which gives a list of significant days in the year for the city of Rome probably drawn up nearly twenty years earlier, in 336. Why this particular date was chosen for the feast has been the subject of some debate among scholars, and there have been two principal schools of thought.

The first, often termed the computation hypothesis, attributed it to the results of ancient attempts to calculate the exact day in the year on which Jesus had actually been born. Although the assumptions and method of reckoning of the early Christians would not be accepted today, they were convinced that the duration of Jesus' human existence must have been an exact number of years, and therefore the date on which he died would have been the same as the date of his conception. Since some of them calculated that he had died on 25 March, this would have placed his conception on the very same date, and his birth exactly nine months later, on 25 December.

The second, often called the 'history of religions' hypothesis, asserted instead that the date had been chosen because it was the occasion of the winter solstice in the Julian calendar and also of a very popular pagan feast at Rome, established by the emperor Aurelian in 274 to celebrate the *dies natalis solis invicti*, the birthday of the invincible sun. After the Peace of Constantine, Christian leaders would have wanted to draw people away from these pagan festivities and point to Christ as the true Sun of Righteousness, and so instituted at Rome the feast of the Nativity on the same date.

It is quite possible that both these factors played a part in the origin of the feast: calculation may have suggested the particular date, but the need to provide a counter-attraction to the temptation for recently converted Christians to continue to participate in the pagan festival probably encouraged the establishment of the Christian observance. We do know that certain other Christian holy days originally emerged precisely as alternatives to pagan celebrations already held on those dates: 1 January, for example, became a Christian day of penitence in several places, and then later a feast of Mary at Rome, because pagans were keeping the date as a festival of the god Janus.

Whatever the reasons for the selection of 25 December, however, it is important to note that the day was thought of as more than just a commemoration of the birthday of Jesus. For instance, the oldest gospel readings associated with the feast at Rome were not only Luke's story of the birth of Jesus but also the beginning of the Gospel of John, with its assertion that 'the Word was made flesh and dwelt among us' (1.14). In other words, what was being celebrated was not just the historical event of the nativity, but belief in the reality of the *incarnation* of the Son of God: hence there was a strong doctrinal or apologetic purpose shaping the festival and not merely a popular piety. Even though the Arian heresy had already been condemned at the Council of Nicea in 325, the fourth century continued to be a period of intense debate about the nature of the person of Christ, and so it is easy to see not only why the establishment of a festival that affirmed his divinity would have seemed a good idea but also why it would later have been taken up enthusiastically in other parts of the Christian world.

6 January

The reasons for the choice of this date in other parts of the early Church are much less clear. At one time it was thought that the eastern provinces of the Roman Empire observed 6 January as the date of the winter solstice in accordance with the ancient calendar of Amenemhet I of Thebes (c. 1996 B.C.), and so again, according to this theory, the Christian feast was established to coincide with that occasion. Recently, however, Thomas Talley has demonstrated that there never was a calendar of Amenemhet I; 6 January was nowhere thought to be the winter solstice; nor is there any strong evidence that it was once the occasion of a widespread pagan festival. He argued that instead the date was arrived at by computation. 6 April had been observed by early Christians in Asia Minor as the annual celebration of the death of Christ, and by the same method of calculation outlined above in relation to 25 December, this practice could easily have given rise to the tradition known to Clement of Alexandria at the end of the second century that 6 January had been the date of the birth of Christ.

On the other hand, what is remarkable about the observance of this festival is that it is not focused on the nativity or the incarnation in every place in which it is encountered. While the nativity (including the visit of the Magi, Matt. 2.1-12) certainly seems to have been its theme in the church at Jerusalem, this was not the case for Christians in Egypt, where 6 January celebrated instead the baptism of Jesus. Elsewhere, there are some indications that the miracle at Cana in Galilee (John 2.1-11) may have been the primary focus.

Talley explained this diversity on the grounds that in all these places the birth of Jesus on 6 January was also understood to mark the beginning of the church's year, and so would have been the occasion when the reading of the particular canonical gospel that was especially associated with each region would have been begun—Mark in Egypt, John in Asia Minor, and Matthew in Jerusalem. In each case, the theme locally connected to the feast occurs at the beginning of the relevant gospel. If true, this suggests that it was the arrangement of the lectionary that determined the character of the various celebrations.

This explanation is not without its difficulties, however. While the baptism of Jesus certainly does occur in the first few verses of Mark's Gospel, in the other two instances the relevant narratives are somewhat further along in the text, and so, if the gospel were being read in order, they would not have been reached until a later occasion. Moreover, evidence from northern Italy in the late fourth century reveals the association of a variety of themes with the feast, including not only the visit of the Magi, the baptism, and the miracle at Cana, but also the feeding of the five thousand and the transfiguration.

This weakens the 'beginning of the gospel' theory somewhat. Calculation of the date of Jesus' birth may account for the emergence of the nativity festival at Jerusalem on this date, and the reading of the beginning of Mark's gospel may well have given rise to the celebration of his baptism in Egypt on the same date.

However, it seems likely that it was attribution of the name *epiphaneia* 'manifestation', to the feast that then attracted the various other local themes to it. It is even possible that there might after all have been a widespread pagan festival involving some form of divine epiphany on this date, in spite of the lack of explicit witness to its existence, and that the Christian feast emerged as a counter-attraction to it and/or as a means of propagating the belief that Christ was the real fulfilment of truths dimly perceived in other religions.

The fusion of traditions

By the same process of harmonization that we have already observed going on with regard to patterns of Christian initiation in the second half of the fourth century, churches also then began to adopt various annual festivals that were already being observed in other places. This eventually brought about the situation where all churches kept both 25 December and 6 January. The first of these became the feast of Christ's nativity everywhere (although including in Eastern churches reference to the visit of the Magi), but the meaning attached to the second date varied considerably. In the East the primary theme of 6 January was the baptism of Christ, although references to the miracle at Cana also occur in later liturgical texts prescribed for the occasion. In Rome and North Africa, however, the focus of the feast was on the visit of the Magi, while elsewhere in the West the theme was the baptism of Jesus, either alone or in conjunction with the other earlier epiphany narratives.

Lent

The origins of this season appear to lie in Egypt, where at least from the beginning of the fourth century if not earlier, there was a forty-day fast, kept in imitation of Jesus' forty-day fast in the wilderness after his baptism (Matt. 4.1–11; Mark 1.12–13; Luke 4.1–13). This annual period of fasting seems to have occurred immediately after January 6, which the Egyptian church observed as the commemoration of the baptism of Jesus. It also appears to have been used as the time of fasting before the baptism of new converts, which consequently took place at the close of the forty-day period, and as the final period of penitential fasting for serious sinners before they were allowed to return to participation in the community's eucharistic worship.

Later in the fourth century we find the churches in other parts of the world also observing a similar forty-day season of fasting, which they doubtless adopted from the Egyptian custom. However, they did not locate it following 6 January but instead immediately before their pre-Easter fast, where at least some of them—notably Rome and North Africa—were already accustomed to hold a pre-baptismal fast in preparation for baptism at Easter.[1] This meant that for those churches which observed only two days of fasting (Friday and Saturday) before the festival, the Lenten season began on the Sunday six weeks before Easter and ended on the Thursday immediately prior to Easter. For the churches of the East, which kept six days of fasting before Easter (from Monday to Saturday), Lent began on the Monday of the seventh week before Easter and ended on the Friday nine days before Easter, with the following Saturday and Sunday as a festal intermission between the two fasts. The church at Alexandria was an exception to this Eastern custom. It apparently made the transition to the pre-Easter position somewhat later than the rest, and when it did so, set its beginning only six weeks before Easter, thus overlapping the six-day pre-Easter fast that it had formerly observed.

Because no church ever fasted on Sundays, and many churches did not fast on Saturdays either (with the sole exception of the Saturday immediately before Easter), the forty-day season always contained less than forty days of actual fasting. Gradually, therefore, various churches began to move its beginning backwards so as to extend its length and produce a full forty days of fasting.

FOR FURTHER READING:
Talley, *The Origins of the Liturgical Year*, Parts 2 & 3.

[1] For Easter baptism, see above, pp. 16–17, 23–4; for the pre-Easter fast, see pp. 82–3.

15. Saints' Days

As we have seen, prior to the fourth century the only annual festival that was universally observed was Easter, with its preparatory fast beforehand and its fifty-day celebration afterwards. The calendars of the various churches would have been filled out with the commemoration of one or more local martyrs on the anniversary of the date on which they had died, but usually termed by early Christians their 'birthday' (in Latin, *natale*). The choice of this particular word indicates their conviction that for those who had suffered and died for the Christian faith, death was the gateway to a new beginning, life eternal in heaven with Christ, in whose suffering they had participated. Unlike other Christians, who were thought to sleep in death until the time of the return of Christ in glory, martyrs were believed to be accorded immediate admittance to the presence of God.

The veneration of martyrs in this way is at least as old as the middle of the second century. Our earliest reference to this custom comes from a contemporary account of the martyrdom of Polycarp of Smyrna at this period. This tells us that, after he had been burned to death,

> we at last took up his bones, more precious than precious stones, and finer than gold, and put them where it was meet. There the Lord will permit us to come together according to our power in gladness and joy, and celebrate the birthday of his martyrdom, both in memory of those who have already contested, and for the practice and training of those whose fate it shall be.[1]

It is important to notice that this early practice was intensely *local*. Churches usually only celebrated the festivals of their own martyrs, and not those of other localities. Moreover, the celebration was held not in the house or other building where the local church normally met, but in the very place where the remains of the martyr were interred. The basis for this custom was the funerary meals of contemporary Greek and Roman society, which were held at the tomb on the deceased person's birthday. In the fourth century Christians began to erect church buildings over the place of burial, in which to hold their celebrations, and the sites often became the objects of popular pilgrimage.

It is also important to observe the significance attached to the physical remains of the martyr, as is evidenced by the extract

---

[1] *Martyrdom of Polycarp* 18.2–3. English translation from Kirsopp Lake, *The Apostolic Fathers* II (Heinemann, London 1913), p. 337.

above from the account of the martyrdom of Polycarp. From the beginning, the cult of the martyrs was closely related to such relics, and this explains in large part why celebrations were slow to spread from one local church community to another: other churches did not possess the remains of the martyr around which to organize a cult. It was only later, in the second half of the fourth century, that the practice began of often moving the mortal remains of martyrs from the original place of burial to a more suitable location in an existing church, especially when the tomb had been a considerable distance away from the city itself. Previously, such a action would have been thought sacrilegious in the pagan society of the period. Yet now this development facilitated the removal of individual relics of the martyr—a small bone, for example—from the rest of the body and transporting it to another city, where it could form the basis of a cult there. In this way, churches gradually began to add to their own calendars festivals of martyrs from other places.

The need for relics also helps to explain why the cult of New Testament saints was generally somewhat slow in developing, since the site of their place of burial was usually at first unknown, and why, when this cult did begin, it was not in the West but in the East, as relics gradually began to be 'found' there. Visits by pilgrims to the Holy Land in the fourth century encouraged this practice, as well as the veneration of Old Testament figures whose tombs were regular stopping-places on the itineraries, although this latter cult did not spread much outside the Eastern churches.

The fourth century also saw the beginnings of the extension of the concept of saints from martyrs alone to other holy men and women. Since the persecution of Christians had now ceased, forms of ascetic life were thought of as constituting a spiritual martyrdom. The noble events of the lives of outstanding ascetic figures were recorded by their disciples, and a cult established after their death. Similarly, bishops often initiated the cult of an illustrious predecessor in their episcopal office, no doubt often in the hope that something similar would be done for them when they eventually died.

We need to bear in mind that what was going on in all this was not the *worship* of the saints themselves. Early Christian theologians were insistent that true worship belonged to God alone, but the saints were to be honoured as faithful disciples of Christ. Moreover, just as Christians might ask especially holy people to pray to God on their behalf during their lifetime, so they continued to ask the saints to intercede for them after death, when they were thought to be in the immediate presence of God and so in a position to be effective advocates for the living.

FOR FURTHER READING:

Peter Brown, *The Cult of the Saints: Its Rise and Function in Latin Christianity* (SCM Press, London & University of Chicago Press 1981).
Michael Perham, *The Communion of Saints* (SPCK, London 1980).

Index